HANDBOOKS OF ARCHAEOLOGICAL HISTORY

THE UNIVERSITY OF NEW MEXICO PRESS, ALBUQUERQUE

# HANDBOOKS OF ARCHAEOLOGICAL HISTORY

*by*

## EDGAR L. HEWETT

*So Live the Works of Men*

ALBUQUERQUE, NEW MEXICO

1938

# PAJARITO PLATEAU AND ITS ANCIENT PEOPLE

PLATE A

TWO KOSA SPRITES BACK OF THE SUN

# Pajarito Plateau and Its Ancient People

*by*

## EDGAR L. HEWETT

PUBLICATION OF
THE UNIVERSITY OF NEW MEXICO
AND
THE SCHOOL OF AMERICAN RESEARCH

UNIVERSITY OF NEW MEXICO PRESS

# TABLE OF CONTENTS

# LIST OF ILLUSTRATIONS

*See page 138 for list of illustrations in Appendix I*

# HANDBOOKS OF ARCHAEOLOGICAL HISTORY

## FOREWORD

If you want to feel the power and pathos of time, roll up in your blankets some night on any one of a hundred mesas, or in any one of a hundred canyons of the old abandoned land of the Pajaritans. The stars that sparkle down on you watched over the cataclysm that rent the nearby mountains some millions of years ago; saw the vast blanket of volcanic ash laid down around the yawning crater, largest on the world's surface; saw the mesas rise out of the chaos, the rifts deepen into gorges; saw vegetation again creep over the ashen landscape, forests slowly wrap the mountain sides in green, and wild life seek timidly the shelter of aspen and pine; saw cliffs and caves shaped by wind and rain; and, at last, saw human life drift quietly in, take up the routine of orderly existence, then quietly flow on into the ocean which we call Time. Listen to the winds that sang through the pines a thousand years ago—melodies that, unknown and unnoticed through silent centuries, have never ceased and never will.

Across the centuries, soft voices ripple in unison with the *ritos* and the gentle winds that stir the cornfields. The shadowy beings that till the fields, climb the cliffs, and chant the rituals that dramatize their simple faith and trustful life seek only to share the ineffable harmony that is all about.

The thunders that break over you and set the yellow cliffs reverberating are the same that told the dreamers of a millenium ago the Trues were above, and would send the rain. The *katsinas* guard the mating of youth and maid and gently lead the old ones along the western trail to the shadowy *Sipophe*. No turmoil here, no questioning the future. None ask, "If a man die shall he live again?" All accept the bounty of the givers of life tranquilly and gratefully. Just beyond the western hills is the land of Sipophe. The Ancients are there. The Trues are always near. Could anyone ask more of life? You, too, can quietly dream yourself into unity with this immutable universe.

13

Forty years ago I came here when the stillness and the mystery of it were undisturbed. I tramped over every mile of it with Indian guides, whose moccasined feet made no sound and left no scars in the deep worn rock trails. Weyima (Antonio Domingo Peña), Potsonutse (Diegito Roybal), Oyegepi (Santiago Naranjo), and Agauono (Juan Gonzales) were a part of the scenery. I, at first, was not, but did my best, and eventually grew into the spirit of it. It took quite a while to make up my mind to disturb the soil that I felt was sacred; longer still to spoil the scene with scientific papers. Even now, as I begin to assemble the notes and papers of years, I am sensible of the futility of a book about a place where all realities have melted into shadows. Who can describe silence and space and time, and a world of only immemorial spirits? Your Indians know all about it, but are too wise to try to utter it. It was never necessary to question these men. As the campfire glowed into the night, an old man's chant quavered out into the spaces; a young man's mating song flowed into the darkness; the drum came out from somewhere, calling the eagles and the buffalo (or at least their impersonators) from the shadows; and the canyon throbbed with the rhythms of the ages. You did not need any "informants." You lived in an esoteric world. When the story-telling began, there was no evasion or restraint. Culture heroes and deities were revealed and discussed, and episodes taken down from the shelves of time where they seemed to be filed as carefully as the material in any other library. It was like "The Uncorking of the Rain Jars" of their own mythologies. That is half the reason why Part One of this book is called "History in Storage." The other half lies under the ruin mounds.

Unless you can sense the unseen world that is mirrored in this book; unless you can restore to these mesas, canyons, and ruined homes the human spirits that moved here through their centuries; unless life comes back to animate these scenes, this will be dull and profitless reading. We hear of *creative writing*. I ask for a few hours of *creative reading*. What the archaeologist can exhibit to you will be a panorama of bleached bones or a pageant of human life, according to the understanding which you and he reach as to your respective parts. Unless you summon a creative imagination to the picture, unless "the stones come to life," the voices of the past are inaudible. If the idea of a "dead" past dominates the scene, then archaeology should be left alone. The loveliest creations of all time can be retrieved from refuse heaps; the most beautiful characters of history can be recalled from a buried past. But it takes two to bring it about; writer and reader must get on common ground.

In this handbook are assembled accounts of explorations and excavations that began on Pajarito Plateau a good many years ago and have continued down to recent times. The substance of some of this has been published before in fugitive papers not now easily accessible. The requirements of a too busy life have prevented publication of detailed, technical reports. This work embraces about all I know that the general reader will care for of this fascinating old region. One merit I can claim for it is that it was learned first-hand. On foot and in the saddle, through days and nights, "where the silence lives," I did the preliminary exploring and mapping, and learned to some extent to see through Indian eyes the region and the ancient life that had pulsated there. Later, with the assistance of eager students, the more systematic work of excavating was done. So you may imagine what this old land has come to mean to me. Little had been done there by way of scientific research prior to my time. It was a new, old region, waiting to give up its story.

Two names that must forever be uppermost in connection with the ancient history of Pajarito Plateau, from the Rito de los Frijoles south to Cochiti, are those of Adolph F. Bandelier and Charles F. Lummis. Bandelier studied the Rito ruins in relation to the Indians of Cochiti pueblo as part of his assignment by the Archaeological Institute of America, beginning in the latter part of 1880 and continuing for several years. One result was his ethnological novel, *The Delight Makers,* which has run through several editions and which still ranks as the best work of fiction ever produced on the Indians of the Southwest. It was done as meticulously as was all his scientific work—the picture of the life of that shadowy time being thoroughly dependable. At the same time every requirement of first-class fiction was observed. Technical reports may be pretty dull reading and usually do not get beyond the circle of readers professionally interested, their writers, as a rule, failing to enable the general reader to visualize times and places and people so as to make the whole business worthwhile. In *The Delight Makers,* Bandelier restored life to the long-silent Rito. A romance, yes. Much romance is as true as a great deal of science, and the Rito is one of the Southwest's romantic spots. The book can be unqualifiedly recommended to the general reader and to university classes in Southwestern ethnology.

Bandelier's purely scientific work, touching upon the Rito and its archaeological and historical relations with Tewa and Keres, is embodied in his "Final Report of Investigations Among the Indians of the Southwestern United States," Part II, published by the Archaeological Institute of America. It is now rather difficult to acquire and would bear re-publication. As the Rito is now a national monument, named in honor of Bandelier, and visited by thousands of travelers annually, the true history of his work there should be known and the exact facts used by the national park lecturers who instruct the traveling public.

Bandelier and Lummis were cronies in the Southwest, later in Peru. For all time to come those who would know the old Southwest must go to the writings of Charles F. Lummis. It got into his soul, and, with his unparalleled gift of language, he put the Southwest into the literature of America. *The Land of Poco Tiempo; Mesa, Canyon and Pueblo;* a dozen other books, magazine articles by the score, and countless editorials in *Land of Sunshine* (afterwards *Out West),* and *The Los Angeles Times,* mirrored the Southwest and its people, Indians and Mexicans. He preëmpted it as his own literary field, and so jealous was he of its reputation, so indignant at any misrepresentation of it by novices or "four-flushers," that he created, and for many years conducted, a department in *Out West* called the "Lion's Den," for the express purpose of throwing terror into the souls of miscreants who fell below his standards in literary or scientific ideals. That his standards were high is witnessed by the fact that the scholarly, meticulous, intolerant Bandelier became his patron saint. To be mauled in the Lion's Den was an experience that the pseudo-scientist or historian hardly cared to survive. Nevertheless, Lummis, with all his eccentricities, was one of the gentlest and most likeable of men;

steadfast in his friendships, obstinate in his convictions, exuberant in his enthusiasms to the point of wild exaggerations, with a mind like a steel trap, and at bottom a character of pure gold. Bandelier with his many faults, greatly over-emphasized by his critics, was equally hard to understand. Misanthropic, suspicious at times of even his best friends, fiercely critical of sham and mediocrity, of vast egotism, tempered with deep and genuine humility, and with all, childlike, generous, and lovable. In his ethnological work he was a too devoted adherent of the principles developed by Lewis H. Morgan (as many biologists have been to Darwinism), but, aside from this, his intellectual independence was extraordinary.

These two men became congenial companions. Whatever they did not like about one another was stated without reserve, privately and publicly, but there was mutual respect and affection between them to the end of life. They were together in the Rito, where Bandelier's scientific interpretations prevailed—but reached only a limited public, while Lummis' literary works went to a wide reading world. I claim some proprietorship in Pajarito Plateau myself, but from the Rito south I keep out of the way. That field belongs to Bandelier and Lummis.

In this book I have again sought to emphasize my conception of archaeology. I believe it to be, potentially, the noblest of sciences. I look upon archaeologists as saviors of human values. They may seem to be doing an infinite amount of puttering over inconsequential things, unworkable nomenclatures, theories of little importance which-ever way they go. They probably are. These are gropings in the wilderness. Eventually, out of the ranks of on-coming youth will emerge those who will look the real problems of man in the face. When our educational institutions cease to trouble young people with so many things that do not matter, and put those who prove themselves free and independent in their thinking up against the vital issues, we may have a science that will overpeer all others. Only a sound science of the past can point the way to a reliable science of the future. We shall not be able to ignore many things that are spurious, many that are ignoble in man's history; but with the stress always upon the genuine, manly traits, with veneration of the godlike achievements which have carried man so far up in his world, archaeology may take and hold the highest place among the humanities. Somewhat belated it came as a science to be pursued by systematic methods. Its pioneers in the West were Powell, Holmes, Alice Fletcher, Fewkes, Putnam, Cushing, and Bandelier. Their contributions to our western archaeology and ethnology remain invaluable to the present day. Southwestern studies may proceed safely along the trails blazed by those masters.

In mentioning the above names, I am simply calling attention to those who are to American archaeology and ethnology what Darwin, Huxley, and Agassiz are to biology. They brought these sciences, the one devoted to the living race, the other to its past, into vital coördination. That should have been done in general anthropology, but it was not. I am confidently expecting our younger students to move the frontiers farther on. But the frontiers must be made secure, and that can only be done by being as exacting as Holmes, as relentless as Hrdlička, in demanding that evidence shall be *evidence* that would stand in court. Guesses and vagaries must not pass for facts. Hypotheses, opinions, estimates are necessary in a science of observation like archaeology, but they must be frankly offered for exactly what they are.

The student of science has no need to be told of the joy of original discovery. The acquisition of knowledge, by any means, is a profound satisfaction. But, without discrediting the value of books and the inspiration of teachers, I may be permitted to hold that the transcendent experience of the student is that of looking upon with his own eyes, or touching with his own hands the original sources from which he may derive knowledge. Herein lies the charm of the great Southwest for the scientist as well as for philosopher and artist. It is an inexhaustible fountain of inspiration. In the Grand Canyon, the Petrified Forest, the great Jemez Crater, the mesas and the mountains, are records of forces which shaped the earth on the most colossal scale known to our planet. The drama of life is no less clearly expressed. Here are plants that adapted themselves to a changing world and survived. By means of delicate instruments in desert laboratories, the response of vegetation to the influences of soil, sunlight, and temperature, every hour in the day and every day in the year, is observed and recorded. Forests tell the story of advance and recession. Tree-rings measure climatic pulsations. An extinct fauna, together with a wealth of living species, tells of the struggle under the inexorable law, "adapt or die."

In this account of Pajarito Plateau and its ancient people, I have tried to give you a picture from our Southwest, to lead you to contemplate the mighty forces which shaped it, to think of the subtle influences that abide in it, which moulded life in its myriad forms and shaped the destinies of the men who inhabited it. These are old, old trails over which we have walked in the Southwest in order to bring the experiences of the past into the life of today. Nature is our surest teacher, and man's place and part are fairly clear.

PART ONE

## HISTORY IN STORAGE

### I. The Friendly Soil

NO IDLE FANCY is the concept of Earth Mother. Wide as the world is the idea that all living things, including man, issued from Mother Earth. No primitive belief is more nearly universal, save that of the Sun (or Sky) Father. Herein is the foundation of all belief in deific powers. Life is seen germinating in the earth, emerging from the earth, dependent upon the earth for maintenance. Earth is seen quickening life, nourishing life, preserving life; at last, taking back into her beneficent keeping all things that have been animated with life and endowed with whatever potency life infuses into unliving material.

The archaeologist works mainly with broken things, with objects shaped by human hands, guided by human minds. But the mind that conceived a utensil for domestic use and directed the hand to give it beauty of form and delicacy of finish; reached beyond the requirements of utility and created a lovely thing which served to delight the senses; endowed a Parthenon with the grace of an exalted spirit that survives through destructive ages—that is the real subject of the archaeologist's quest.

Ancient monuments fascinate because of their builders, and builders are interesting for what they wrought under the urge of creative mind. Who? When? Whither? are the questions with which the archaeologist challenges the refuse heaps, scattered potsherds, and broken shafts, to tell of the builders who came and lived and went their way into the templed past. Only as they are reflections of minds and spirits are ruins of importance. Only as they tell the story of man striving toward his manhood do they become landmarks to be cherished and venerated.

Now it is a mystifying thing that man, presumably the end product of all nature's evolutionary endeavors, creator of all the beautiful and majestic cultural products of his world, should at the same time be the most brutal destroyer. Let a people create a palace of beauty, a city of delight, a country of loveliness, a cultural world which would seem to be the supreme objective of human effort, and another people must do its fiendish best to blast it from the earth. Let life become tranquil, happy, abundant in all that is most desirable in existence, and man rises up to crush it into poverty or utter annihilation—usually under pretense of righting wrong or restoring order. "They left a desert and they called it peace." Pursuing his enemy to extinction and himself to exhaustion has been man's usual course throughout history—a process that is working mightily at the present moment. Witness Germany! Japan! Italy hesitating at the Rubicon!

Fortunately, it is usually the male moiety of the human species that goes forth with rifle, machine gun, cannon, hand grenade, to devastate. Woman follows up, salvaging from the battlefield such wreckage as she can, determined that the life which issued from her own being shall not perish from the earth. Life marches on with the balance somewhat in favor of survival, but with an appalling amount of destruction. But here beneficent nature steps in to save culture from its creator-destroyer; even to rescue man from himself. That is what saves the archaeologist from despair. With what uncanny intelligence nature gets to work with wind, sand, and jungle to protect life's achievements! Works of Phidias, statues of unnamed Maya masters, will be cracked into fragments and built into pigsties if man is given a little time. I have seen men, too lazy to get in out of the rain, working—actually working—to destroy a venerable landmark. Our generation has witnessed nations that suppose themselves to have reached the apex of civilization throwing all their resources of property and human life into the destruction of earth's most precious possessions. Man does not hesitate to put out the torch that has lighted humanity for a thousand years.

Nature quietly, patiently, goes to work. Over the ruins of cities winds pile the friendly soil. Rains undercut the foundations of walls and columns so that they may fall and be concealed from the vandals. Roofs collapse; windows and doors and corridors are blocked with dirt; marble halls are filled with debris so that they may not be used for cowsheds or burned into lime. Nature is relentless in her protective work. She will convert fertile lands into desert wastes, cultivated valleys into impenetrable jungles, to the end that the things of man's spiritual past may be saved for the life of the future. Infinite wisdom! Infinite patience! Infinite affection! What to Mother Nature is the brooding of a thousand years if it insures the immortality of the human spirit? Nature waits long and lovingly for the archaeologist—him of the pick, trowel, and spade—tries him out with desert dust and jungle fever; rewards him graciously, once in a while lavishly, with fruits of the toil that built men's souls in ages past and insured to them a victorious future.

History is stored away in the archives of Mother Earth. Some of it has been printed in books and filed on library shelves, but the greater part, written unconsciously in things fashioned for use and in things that ministered only to the satisfaction of the spirit, is under the soil. All these nature has patiently gathered and stored away to await hands to pick up the broken threads and begin to weave anew the patterns of life that must be woven to completion, in spite of wars or vandals or other obstacles—in spite of time itself. A goal seems to have been set for man's endeavors. The evidences of it are mainly stored under the friendly soil, material for archaeological history. This kind of history has decided advantages over the documentary. It was written unconsciously; therefore, is free from the egotisms, prejudices, and personalities of deliberately planned biography or autobiography. Nature has cared little about the preservation of the gross or vulgar. The flower of culture has survived for the enrichment of life. She does not exploit the worst of the human traits; she conserves the best. Here is a lesson for the documentary historian. There has been much tendency of late years to knock the immortal ones of history from their pedestals. It is an unfortunate trend. The historian who conceives it to be his duty to de-bunk the world's greatest characters is a public enemy. We all know that these were human beings, that they possessed the characteristics common to all mankind. What we want to perpetuate is the energy in every great soul that moved the frontiers of mankind forward.

## II. LORE OF THE LIVING

Not to the friendly soil alone must the archaeologist go for the recovery of human history put away in storage. The racial mind is likewise a vast depository of records to tell the story of man through the ages, usually thought of as unrecorded. Events happen in primitive society which, in the absence of true writing, must be embalmed in racial memory. By *true writing* I mean the expression of thought in sentences by means of literary characters. All the indigenous Americans were non-literary people. The ancient Pueblos used rock pictures and art symbols as a mode of expression. The Aztecs had an elaborate system of pictography which they used in naming places, deities, etc. The Maya developed a system of hieroglyphics mainly for calendrical purposes and to some extent for depicting their pantheon. But neither ancient Pueblo, Aztec, nor Maya ever wrote a sentence in literary form or characters. True writing may be regarded as non-existent in ancient America.

But no race lives without cherishing the deeds of its ancestors, without wanting a record of its own time to be handed on to the coming generations. The acts of fathers and mothers, especially fathers, are recounted with pride and affection at primitive firesides. Therein is one of the bonds of family life. Within a few generations outstanding deeds of ancestors become community traditions to fire the imagination of youth. As time goes on, culture heroes grow out of racial memories, ennobling the past as earth-gods. Finally, they are enthroned on Olympus or in Valhalla as veritable deities. Ancestor veneration is a perfectly human trait, and there is nothing more human than the process by which mythologies grow. Outstanding achievements among fellow men become tradition; the captain of tradition becomes a legendary hero, from which stage it is an easy step to demigod.

Tribal or community movements are always impressed strongly upon the collective mind. As long as accounts of these are not too remote, they may be regarded as fairly reliable tradition—not to be accepted literally, but as embodying shadowy facts of folk migration. Examples of this are the traditions of the Tewa with reference to moves from the Pajarito Plateau to Rio Grande Valley sites, and those of the Keres as recorded by Charles F. Lummis in "The Wanderings of Cochiti," *The Land of Poco Tiempo*. Partly in this category are *The Books of Chilan Balam* of Yucatan.

Tradition fades into legend and, after long lapse of time, chiefs, caciques, war captains, who have actually led community movements, become legendary heroes who conduct their people through all sorts of dangers and hardships to new lands. Montezuma, historic priest-chief of the Aztecs, was thus lifted from Anahuac to the Rio Grande Valley. Nearly all Pueblo villages have their Montezuma legends; the *Annals of the Cakchiquels* of Guatemala are largely migration legends.

With time, long ages of it, legend fades into myth. Migration myths are among the cherished intellectual possessions of most primitive people—certainly of all indigenous communities of the American Southwest. Along with these evidences of the play of fancy, characteristic of all esthetic people, which has given rise to most of the world's great literature, grows up the vast body of mythology which for its origins harks back over the long road of tribal experience above outlined, but which grows from generation to generation as the primitive myth-makers weave their fireside stories into the community culture. Mythology grows among non-literary people as fiction does among the literati of civilization.

No sharp distinction is made between myth and folk tale, though it would be convenient if these could be differentiated. The "Outlines of Zuñi Creation Myths," by Frank Hamilton Cushing, and tales of the Hero Twins—culture heroes of the stature of demigods—may be classed as matured mythology. Likewise are the Quetzalcoatl myths of the Aztecs, Kukulcan of the Maya, and the Maya-Quiché Popul Vuh. Folk tales might be restricted to stories of the Jack-the-Giant-Killer sort and the animal yarns, like Brer Rabbit, in which the Pueblo culture of the Rio Grande Valley is so rich. *(See:* Lummis' *Pueblo Indian Folk-Stories,* some of Cushing's Zuñi folk tales, and some of the tales in my *Ancient Life in the American Southwest.)*

No claim is made that more than a small part of the non-literary material above described is to be given the status of veritable literary history, nor is the general pattern laid down to be accepted as a hard and fast evolutionary series. It may be asserted, however, that in community and tribal tradition, legend, myth, folk tale, there is an enormous amount of human history of the cultural sort stored away, which, with discriminating study, throws light upon the past of non-literary peoples. Even seemingly frivolous animal tales have significance in relation to the little-understood subject of totemism, and running through many of them is the vein of quaint, homely philosophy which is worthy of serious consideration in evaluating the folk intelligence.

There can be no discounting the service of mythology in reflecting the spiritual life. So intimate is the relation of man to nature in the Southwest that the major part of human culture is to be looked upon as man's interpretation of his world. Culture heroes, even if of the stature of demigods, and even immaterial deific powers, must reside somewhere. Ethnogeography reveals the Pueblo Indian's understanding of the world about him. *(See:* John P. Harrington, "The Ethnogeography of the Tewa Indians," *Twenty-ninth Annual Report,* Bureau of American Ethnology—the most complete and authentic thing of its kind that has been published.) But a Pueblo cosmography is equally vital and has not been written—cannot be, in fact, until much more is known, though Harrington made a good start at it. We must get it mainly through oral information, dramatic ceremonies, from pottery ornamentation, rock pictography, and kiva paintings. The recently uncovered frescoes at Kuaua, ancient Tiguex town on the west bank of the Rio Grande, opposite Bernalillo, a preliminary study of which will be presented in the forthcoming handbook, *Archaeological History of the Rio Grande Valley,* constitute the most valuable record of its kind that has been discovered in the Southwest, if not in all America.

Nature, from age to age, has been storing under friendly soil the unwritten history of man. Unconsciously, man himself has been filing the records of his intellectual and spiritual life in the archives of racial mind. Does this suggest a new science—paleopsychology? If so, let us drop it *pronto.* We have too much unbaked nomenclature already. Archaeology is a perfectly adequate term.

PART TWO

MESAS, CANYONS, AND RUINS

I. NATURE'S WORK

OME YEARS ago, I proposed the name Pajarito Plateau
for the eastern side of the watershed of the Jemez
mountain range. (The larger term, Jemez Plateau,
embraces both sides of the watershed.) It was generally accepted and is applied to the region lying east of
the foothills, limited on the east by the Rio Grande,
north by the Rio Chama, and south by the Cañada de
Cochiti. It varies from ten to twenty miles in width,
is about forty miles long and roughly crescent-shaped.
It is boldly defined on all sides. The mountains on the
western rim, known as the Jemez, also as the Valles
range, are from nine thousand to eleven thousand feet
in altitude. The sides which rise from the valleys
present varying aspects. In places, the rim has been
broken by torrential erosion into huge fragmentary
escarpments, rising abruptly from two hundred to
fifteen hundred feet. Again, in places it is continuous for some miles
except as cut through here and there by narrow, deep gorges through
which the torrents of flood season find their way to the Rio Grande.
A third aspect of the margin is one in which recent basaltic extrusions
occur along the broken rim. In places, as White Rock Canyon, the
margin of the plateau is extended to the river with no space between
for even an Indian trail. Again, it recedes from the river a distance
of perhaps three-quarters of a mile.

The entire plateau was covered originally with a sheet of grayish
yellow volcanic tufa, varying in thickness from one hundred to one
thousand feet. This material came, millions of years ago, from the vast
crater of the Jemez range lying between Mount Pelado and Mount

27

Redondo. I speak of this enormous depression as a crater, on the authority of the United States Geological Survey, aware, however, that some geologists are not satisfied with this interpretation of it. It is the Valle Grande of the older maps, having a long axis of about eighteen miles and short diameter of twelve. If it has been correctly identified, it is the largest crater on the globe. Figure 1 is from the relief map in the Geological Survey in Washington; the arrow indicates El Valle Grande. In superficial appearance it certainly meets every requirement of a volcanic crater, and incidentally, gives New Mexico something to brag about. The floor of the depression is a grassy plain, broken in places by basaltic and tufaceous hills. The broken rim is heavily forested with pine and spruce (Fig. 2). Whichever way the dispute of the geologists turns out, this is one of the natural wonders of the Southwest. If a true crater, it is to volcanic phenomena what Grand Canyon is to erosion and Carlsbad to cavern formation.

In places, particularly in the older strata, the material surrounding the depression consisted of a mixture of water, ash, and cinders of the consistency of mud, forming, when indurated, a compact, stratified, brownish mass. Another form of the deposit was that of a dry ash, to be seen in light, porous, non-stratified masses, conspicuous by their glaring whiteness. A third form, and this is predominant throughout the plateau, is the thick, non-stratified sheet, tending to columnar structure, ranging from a light, porous, gray pumice to fairly compact yellow tufa, in places approaching the hardness of sandstone, carrying a high percentage of silicious material in the form of minute crystals. It is with this form that we have to do in archaeological studies. Rudely dressed from the irregular blocks into which it is readily broken, it furnished a durable and easily worked building material for the inhabitants of the plateau through a long period of time. Caves, both natural and artificial, in the perpendicular cliffs, also afforded comfortable and secure abodes with but little labor.

Looking from an eminence across a typical area, it is obvious that the volcanic blanket originally formed a continuous, level covering for the entire plateau. Less than 10 per cent of it has withstood the erosive forces of past ages. These remnants stand out boldly in

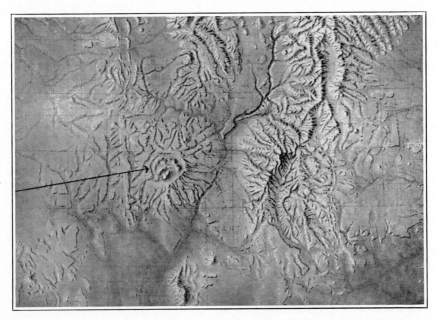

FIG. 1. RELIEF MAP, JEMEZ AND SANGRE DE CRISTO RANGES; EL VALLE GRANDE

FIG. 2. TYPICAL VIEW OF PAJARITO PLATEAU

FIG. 3.   TENT ROCKS WEST OF OTOWI

FIG. 4.   A DISTANT VIEW OF OTOWI RUINS

long, narrow mesas *(potreros)* pointing toward the river. The southern walls are usually almost perpendicular. The northern faces vary from gentle to abrupt slopes, rarely presenting perpendicular walls of more than a few feet in height. Thousands of caves, located, for the most part, in the upper ledges of the mesas, originally started by water erosion, are still in constant process of enlargement through action of the winds.

At the base of every one of these potreros is a sloping talus, in places extending halfway up the height of the mesa. The incline of this is, in some places, very steep, in others, a gentle slope extending far out to the flood plain below. The upper part of the talus is full of huge blocks of the tufa which have fallen away from the rim of the mesa. This breaking down is continually going on, the result of moisture and frost. Usually when the cleavage occurs, the mass slips down, partially burying itself in the soft talus unless the incline is very steep. This has gone on before, during, and since the period of human occupation of the cliffs. Evidences of earthquake activity of moderate violence are revealed in this connection. In places, enormous blocks of the tufa, which, under the ordinary conditions of weathering, would have slipped from the cliff and been embedded in the soft talus, are found at considerable distance beyond the foot of the slope on the level flood plain; this, too, where the precipice is quite low and the slope gentle. This journey could have been accomplished only through some unusual initial energy that is explicable on no other theory than that of earthquake action. Good examples of this are to be seen in the tributaries of Pajarito Canyon.

The plateau is forested heavily on the western side, yellow pine being the most prevalent and most valuable tree. Englemann spruce, white fir, and red fir are plentiful on the upper slopes. There are extensive groves of aspen in the high gulches and on protected slopes. The central zone, which includes the formerly inhabited part, is lightly covered with pine, piñon, and juniper, interspersed with many small, open, grassy parks. The large area in the east central part is devoid of timber. There are many small valleys and some broad, level mesas which, if irrigable, would make excellent agricultural land. Permanent water exists only on the western side. Only one of the many streams which originate on the slopes of the mountains, the Rito de los Frijoles, carries its water to the Rio Grande unfailingly throughout the year.

No considerable part of the formerly inhabited area can now be farmed because of lack of water during the greater part of the year. The country may be characterized as arid, but not desert. It is a region of beautiful scenery, delightful climate, and, in places, fertile soil, uninhabited at the present time solely because of lack of rainfall and water for irrigation.

Between Santa Clara Creek and El Rito de los Frijoles are thousands of acres of arable lands, the largest body lying between Pajarito Canyon and El Rito de los Frijoles. Here the high, tongue-like mesas protruding toward the river, with broad, timbered valleys between, are replaced by a spacious tableland, the Mesa del Pajarito, which at first sight appears to be a continuous expanse partially covered with pine, piñon, and juniper. It is, however, deeply cut at intervals by narrow, impassable canyons. With the exception of the part bordering on the Rio Grande, which is exceedingly rugged, much of the mesa is covered with fertile soil. Large areas of it were cultivated by the ancient inhabitants, as shown by numerous vestiges of former tillage. The largest body of anciently cultivated land is on the southern part of this mesa. There are also areas of similar character about the ruined villages of Tsirege, Navawi'i, Navahu'u, and Puyé. On the top of a high mesa south of the Guajes, named Mariposa Mesa because of the fields of Mariposa lillies growing there, are several hundred acres of good land that was cultivated in ancient times. This has not been reforested since abandoned for agriculture, as has much of the Mesa del Pajarito.

The country is poor in natural food products. A few berries, wild cherries, and plums are found in the lower canyons and are prized by the Indians. There is some scrub oak, the acorns of which would furnish an appreciable amount of food. The most abundant food of this class is the seed of the piñon (Pinus edulis), which is used by the Indians. Fish are not plentiful. Some trout are found in the mountain streams, but the Pueblo Indians fish very little. The country is rather poor in game. Deer are more rare here than in northern New England. Bears are seldom seen. There are a few wild turkeys, but the

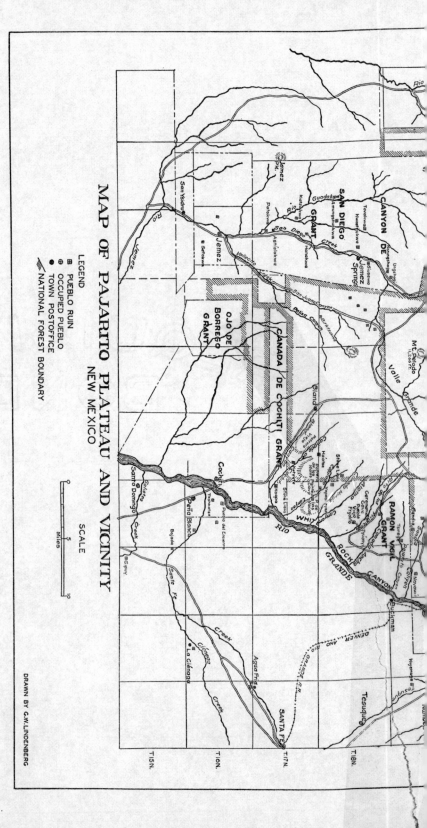

MAP OF PAJARITO PLATEAU AND VICINITY
NEW MEXICO

LEGEND
■ PUEBLO RUIN
⊕ OCCUPIED PUEBLO
● TOWN POSTOFFICE
▨ NATIONAL FOREST BOUNDARY

SCALE
0    5    10
Miles

FIG. 5

DRAWN BY G.W.LINDENBERG

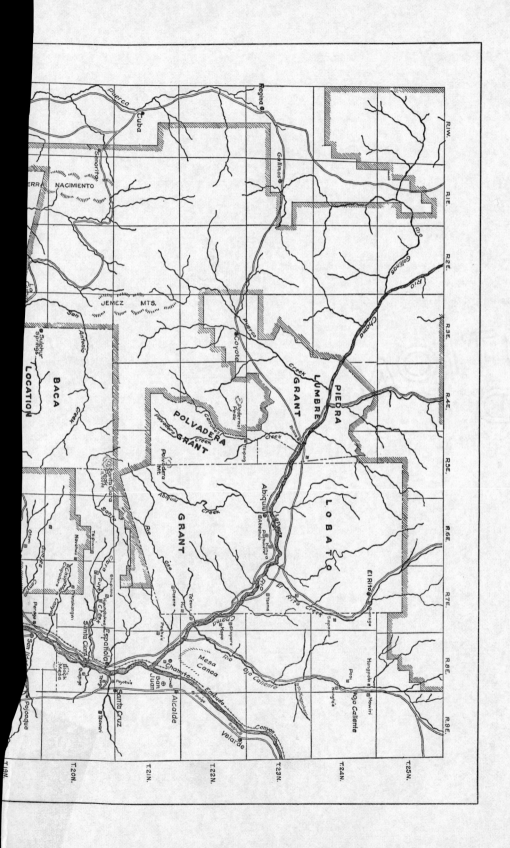

country is almost devoid of birds. There is an exceedingly rich insect fauna. I have never seen elsewhere such swarms of butterflies. There are many lizards, tarantulas, and centipedes. Rattlesnakes occasionally appear on the mesas and in the Rio Grande Valley, being unpleasantly numerous in White Rock Canyon. Bats frequent the crevices in the cliffs. Occasionally locusts appear in great numbers. These were used for food by the Indians quite generally in earlier times.

The above description applies to Pajarito Plateau of today, of forty years ago, and of a thousand years ago, excepting for the better water supply of the earlier time. Desiccation has been going on for a long while. When it reached the point where human subsistence was no longer possible, or at least too difficult to warrant further occupation, no one knows. My surmise has always been that the Pueblo Indians ceased to be cliff dwellers during the period of seven to eight centuries ago. This was not entirely a guess, being based mainly on Indian tradition. Recent tree-ring studies do not point to any great change in this estimate. There is nothing to indicate sudden emigration. It probably went on for a century or so as life in the cliff country became harder and the adjacent Rio Grande Valley more inviting. We find no such evidence of abrupt exodus here as we do in Chaco Canyon *(see: The Chaco Canyon and Its Monuments)* on the other side of the Continental Divide. The climatic changes of the past four hundred years in the Rio Grande Valley, of which we have documentary history, have not been radical. There has been rather sad local change on Pajarito Plateau during my recollection, owing to the reckless deforestation that took place before our present efficient National Forest Service got into action. It will take a generation or two, but this can probably be corrected. It surely can be if nature is continuously assisted by intelligent reforestation, and if our National Park Service adopts the principle that the best thing to do about a sublime piece of scenery is to leave it alone and see that vandals leave it alone.

## II. The Coming of Man

The advent of the human species in this region is obscure. No vast antiquity is indicated, as compared with the antiquity of man in Europe. We cannot postulate a paleolithic or neolithic man in the

New World, or follow any Old World pattern in classification. Any dogmatic statement as to time of occupation in the major culture centers of the Southwest is premature, and schemes of chronological sequence in cultural developments are tentative. For all practical purposes we may begin the study of man in this region with the ancient Pueblos and cliff dwellers. Remains which some interpret as evidences of earlier stocks are to be considered, and their meaning and relative importance held in abeyance awaiting more convincing data.

Nothing has been established as to whence came this first outstanding culture of the Southwest. In general, Pueblo tradition points toward migration from the north. The remote infiltration of the indigenous American people from Asia, by way of the Bering waters, and a culture level at the time of arrival on this continent comparable to that of neolithic Europe, is generally accepted by Americanists. These people arrived and continued without practical knowledge of metals. Therefore, while exploring and settling a vast continent, they remained low in material achievements. In many elements of culture they surpassed their European contemporaries.

It would seem that some ancient culture wave, traversing the Rio Grande Valley in remote times, must have thrown off detachments which lodged in the canyons and cliffs of this Southwestern plateau. The cause of the unique localization of these bands is not, at first, clear. It is unlikely that motives of defense directed the choice, as would at first seem indicated, for much evidence tends to show that the modern predatory tribes—Navaho, Apache, and Ute—arrived in the Southwest in comparatively recent times. The construction of the great defensive community houses of the Pajaritans belongs to the latest epoch of their history. For a long period they were dispersed over the plateau. This was the epoch of the "small houses," of which several thousand have been counted in this region. There is both archaeologic and physiographic evidence that the earliest inhabitants arrived at a time when climatic conditions were radically different from those of the present. The proof of slow, progressive desiccation of the Southwest is abundant. The plateau has lain uninhabited for centuries because of the scarcity of water. The great communities, representing the last stages of habitation, clustered about the gradually failing springs. The earlier small house ruins are found

FIG. 6. A VIEW THROUGH EL VALLE GRANDE

FIG. 7. INTERIOR OF A CAVE DWELLING, TYÚONYI

Fig. 8.  Stone Axes From Pajaritan Excavations

everywhere, indicating a climatic condition favorable to agriculture. It would thus appear that the reason for selection of the plateau as a place of abode by those bands which first settled here was simply that in those times this now desiccated tableland afforded more favorable conditions for subsistence than did the adjacent valley of the Rio Grande—a condition now reversed.

Leaving the conjectures of the archaeologists for the certainties of the Pueblo Indians, we are not troubled with contradictory evidence nor cross currents of beliefs. They *know.* Men and animals were born in an underworld. They emerged from it by way of a lake called Sipophe. After several unsuccessful attempts, they managed it by climbing up a great spruce tree that extended up through the water like a ladder. You see a reminiscence of this in the long ladder that extends up out of the kiva, far above the roof. The spirit people "go west" on their journey to a kiva-like place, *Weyima,* in the underworld, passing through the lake of Sipophe (or Sipope), where there are many spirits in the waters. It seems that I accidentally discovered the lake that figures so vitally in Tewa mythology, on a camping trip in 1892. At that time I knew nothing of its significance. Dr. John P. Harrington, in his Tewa ethnogeography *(Twenty-ninth Annual Report,* Bureau of American Ethnology, pp. 567-568) says:

*Sipop'e* is a brackish lake situated in the sand dunes north of Alamosa, Colorado. It is east of Mosca, a station on the railroad which runs from Alamosa to Silverton, and west of the Sierra Blanca. . . . This lagoon was visited by Dr. E. L. Hewett in 1892, who kindly furnished the following note taken from his diary at that time:

June 27, 1892. Camped over night on the summit of Mosca Pass on the way to Alamosa. During the forenoon drove down the steep western slope and near evening camped not far from a ranch house on the eastern side of the San Luis valley. There appears to be here a fertile strip between the foot of the mountain and the sand dunes of the valley. Here and there the soil seems very marshy and in places there is something very much like quicksand. One of my ponies suddenly dropped to the belly in a moist place by the roadside.

June 28, 1892. The trip from last night's camp to Alamosa was by a very little used road across the sand dunes. These are enormous hills of continually shifting sand. I am told that these dunes constantly change position, shifting a considerable distance in a few days. Soon after noon, to the west of a group of dunes, we passed a small lake of very black, forbidding looking water. It looks much like the small crater lakes south of Antonito but is not in a volcanic district. I could form no idea of the depth of it, but should think it quite deep. It is probably 100 yards across. The water is very offensive. Around the shore is a continuous line of dead cattle. The place interests me very much. There are no settlements within a distance of many miles, and the only information I could gain concerning it was from a very garrulous old man (the only human being that we saw during the day), who with his team of oxen pulled us out of an old irrigating ditch in which we were stalled for an hour or more in the afternoon. He lived up on the mountain side (Sierra Blanca) and had for many years. He had seen the lake and claimed that it never dried up: that many cattle died from drinking the water every dry season. . . .

The location of *Sipop'e* is generally and definitely known to the Tewa.

•

In proposing the name which is now generally accepted for the plateau lying between the Jemez Mountains and the Rio Grande and extending from the Chama Valley to Cañada de Cochiti, I chose the central geographical feature of the area, i.e., the Pajarito Canyon (Spanish *pajarito,* "a little bird," a sparrow). The Tewa name, Tsirege, is applied to a cliff ruin on the northern rim of this canyon, in which, as well as in the neighboring village sites, I have made numerous excavations. These investigations made known a new region and a culture which, from the community on which the type is based, I named the Pajaritan.

The archaeological remains of this culture are scattered over almost the whole of the Pajarito Plateau. There were several foci of population, the Puyé, the Pajarito, and the Rito de los Frijoles. The relationship between these groups remains to be established, but certain common characteristics indicate connection as close as that now existing between the Tewa villages of San Juan, Santa Clara, and San Ildefonso, though it does not necessarily follow that the same language was spoken in all the settlements. These groups afford facilities for the study of the development of culture through a long period

FIG. 9. KIVA IN CEREMONIAL CAVE, TYÚONYI—AFTER EXCAVATION

FIG. 10. TALUS RUINS, RITO DE LOS FRIJOLES

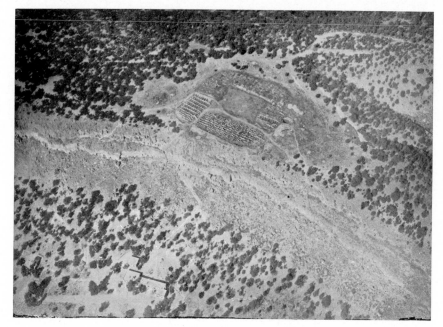

FIG. 11. AERIAL VIEW OF PUYÉ

FIG. 12. OTOWI RUINS

of time. The geographical isolation was such as to induce definite, homogeneous development. That this isolation was well preserved is shown in the homogeneity of both the physical type and the cultural remains. In the art of the Pajaritans we may read several centuries of their history. It is pre-Spanish, the excavations having yielded no vestige of European influence, and so distinctly does it reflect the culture in which it was produced that a specimen of pottery from this region is as unmistakable to the trained eye as is anything Greek, Etruscan, or Egyptian.

The diffusion of the ancient Pajaritan population in small house communities might seem to indicate a social organization different from that existing among the people of the later great community houses where the system was the prototype of the modern Pueblos. Such, however, is not the case. In the dispersed small house communities it seems fairly clear that the basic principles of tribal structure that govern in Pueblo organization today were fully developed. There was apparently lacking only the element of dual organization, a social phenomenon which attended the coming together of numerous clans into great communities. This type of genetic aggregation persists among the Pueblos today. It seems probable that in the small house communities the groupal unit was the clan, and the basic social fact the matriarchal system, by virtue of which domestic authority resided in the mother. The fundamental fact of the religious order in the modern pueblos is the dual hierarchy, with authority lodged in two priests, the summer cacique and the winter cacique, who have charge of the ceremonials of their respective seasons. *(Cacique* is a Haitian word which was used extensively by early chroniclers to designate the priest-chiefs of the mainland throughout America; it was incorporated into the Spanish language with this significance.) This system would develop along with the movement toward larger and closer community aggregation, but that the elements of it existed in the small house communities is indicated in the house remains. The structural germ of every house group was the kiva, the ceremonial chamber that is found in all the community houses of the Rio Grande and San Juan valleys. This was the clan sanctuary, the place set aside, before the first stone of the dwelling was laid, for prayer and religious rites.

No other object in Southwestern archaeology is of greater interest than these subterranean sanctuaries. Everywhere on Pajarito Plateau we find the kiva as the nucleus of the settlement. In southeastern Utah, also, the circular underground kiva is conspicuous in every ruin group. The evidences in Utah, Colorado, and New Mexico point to the kiva as the germ of every pueblo. On the testimony of reliable old men, it seems that the first act of a clan was to locate its sanctuary and around it extend the living rooms. The small community ruins scattered over Pajarito Plateau seem to confirm this. With the formation of the great communities it would seem that a new feature of tribal organization developed, namely, that of the dual hierarchy, *summer people* and *winter people,* and with this came the dual kiva system, a sanctuary for each division of the tribe, the point around which the settlement could grow. In it was centered all that was vital to the life and happiness of the people. It was the place of silence, the sanctuary to which those charged with the religious functions of the clan retired for thought, for prayer, for offerings, for sacrifice. It was the place for the performance of secret rites and preparation for public ceremonials. In gathering about the *sipapu,* men approached the Earth Mother; they sought the sources of ancient wisdom; they were at the portal whence life itself emerged. In the kiva of the Rio Grande clans and the observances clustering about it, we have symbolized the Pueblo conception of human birth, the origin of life, and the ordering of human conduct. In the foregoing I am giving the interpretations of Pueblo priests of the older time. The explanations of the younger generation are almost worthless. Thus when it is said that there are no clan kivas in the Rio Grande region and that such did not formerly exist, you may be certain that the information is erroneous.

In Pueblo organization today, the clan kiva has almost disappeared. It still remains at Taos, but at San Juan, Santa Clara, San Ildefonso, Nambé, and Cochiti, only tribal kivas remain. There is the kiva of the summer people and the kiva of the winter people. In some cases one of these is subterranean or semi-subterranean, the other wholly above ground. Both round and rectangular forms exist. The religious functions of the tribe are, as above stated, in the hands of two priests, the summer cacique and the winter cacique. Each one has charge of the ceremonials pertaining to his season, and each officiates in the sanctuary pertaining to that division. The history of this dual organization is not known. That it existed in the later stages of Pajaritan culture cannot be doubted.

In connection with the uses of the kiva among the Pueblos, it is interesting to note the following parallel in Pawnee ritual. I quote from Alice C. Fletcher's study of the Hako:

The first stanza of the second part calls the people to give heed to Ku-sha-ru, a place set apart for sacred purposes. Concerning Ku-sha-ru, the old priest said: "The first act of man must be to set apart a place that can be made holy and be consecrated to Ti-ra-wa, a place where a man can be quiet and think about the mighty unseen power."

. . . the first stanza of the first part made mention of A-wa-hok-shu, the holy place, the abode of Ti-ra-wa, whence life was given to man through the intermediary powers. The first stanza of the second part directs that man should set apart a holy place, where his thoughts could ascend to the life-giving Ti-ra-wa.

The old priest further explained: "We are taught that before a man can build a dwelling, he must select a place and make it sacred, and then about that consecrated spot he can erect a dwelling where his family can live peacefully. Ku-sha-ru represents the place where a man can seek the powers and where the powers can come near to him."

•

There is here significant similarity between the Pueblo kiva as the essential nucleus of a settlement and the "sacred place" of the Pawnee.

The story of man on the Pajarito Plateau is one of adaptation to a peculiarly definite and elemental environment. Obvious everywhere is the urge to live, to reproduce, to survive; and the efforts put forth to that end constitute a fascinating chapter in the history of human arts, industries, social structure, and beliefs. Running through the amazing story, like a golden thread on which the fabric is woven, is the idea of the potency of the environment. Inhospitable as it seems, it yielded to man his food through some centuries, nourished his culture, stimulated his spiritual life.

### III. Grouping of the Ancient Population

The distribution of the ancient people over the Pajarito Plateau was described by me in a publication of the Bureau of American Ethnology *(Bulletin* 32), and in my work, *Les Communautés Anciennes Dans le Désert Américain.* As little has been added to our knowledge of the region subsequent to those publications, the account here given will be, in part, the same. We will begin on the north with the ruins of the Chama drainage.

The Rio Chama enters the Rio Grande just below the village of Chamita, about one mile southwest of the Tewa pueblo of San Juan. It forms the watershed for that portion of northern New Mexico which lies between the Rio Grande and the Continental Divide. From its mouth to above Abiquiu it is closely bordered on the south by the rim of the volcanic plateau which rises abruptly to heights of from two hundred to one thousand feet, while, on the north, there is an open valley broken up by small isolated mesas and truncated cones. Above Abiquiu, the river flows for many miles through a picturesque gorge. The country on both sides is rough and broken.

The entire area is rich in archaeological remains. Above Abiquiu, are both cliff dwellings and pueblo ruins, stone being the building material used. From Abiquiu down, pueblos only are found. With the exception of those at Abiquiu and Chamita all these are prehistoric. A succession of large pueblos occupied commanding sites on the northern rim of the plateau overlooking the Chama. These will be described in the order of their occurrence ascending the river.

About four miles above the confluence of the Chama with the Rio Grande, a chain of detached fragments of the great black Mesa Canoa crosses over to the south side of the river and extends for some miles southwestward. On the top of one of these fragmentary mesas, about one mile south of the river, stood the village of *Poshu'u* (squash projection—stem). Its ruins are probably five hundred feet above the level of the river. The pueblo was constructed of adobe with large, variable blocks of basalt in the foundations. It consisted of three buildings so placed as to partially inclose an irregular quad-rangle. The extreme length of the longest side is 421 feet. There are two circular, subterranean kivas within the court. About one hundred yards south of the pueblo is the ruin of a circular kiva fifty feet in diameter which was in part subterranean and in part built of basalt blocks of varying size, conglomerate, and sandstone, carried above ground to a height of eight to ten feet. About two hundred yards east are the ruins of a building similarly constructed which bears evidence of having been used as a shrine. In this structure big blocks or slabs of stone set on edge were used in the walls, and the general form is that of shrines still in use among the Tewa. It is thirty-five feet in diameter, being considerably larger than the shrines now in use. The pottery of this ruin is similar to that of the ruins found further to the south. While there is evidence of the use of corn, there was no possibility of agriculture in the immediate vicinity. The nearest land that could have been farmed is about one mile away.

*Te'ewi'i* (little cottonwood gap[1]) is an extensive ruin situated on the rim of the mesa overlooking the valley just below the junction of the Rio Oso with the Chama. It is about one-quarter mile south of the river. The bluff on which it stands is approximately two hundred feet high. The pueblo was built of adobe with some lava blocks in the foundations. It is now reduced to low mounds. There were two large adjoining quadrangles, or the pueblo might be described as having been built in one long rectangle divided by cross walls into two courts. The length of the rectangle is 525 feet and the extreme width 210 feet. Within and contiguous to the pueblo are ten circular, subter-ranean kivas, and a few yards to the east is a ruined shrine of circular form eight feet in diameter, built of lava blocks set on edge.

*Kunya* (turquoise) is a large pueblo ruin located on a conical hill some 150 feet high and overlooking the Chama at a point known as La Puente, about three miles below Abiquiu. It was visited by Yarrow in 1874 and was described by Bandelier in 1880. This pueblo covered a greater area than any other in the immediate vicinity of the Chama. It was an adobe structure with about the same amount of rubble in the foundations as the modern Tewas use in the building of their houses.

---

[1] A "wi'i" is a narrow, slightly depressed (saddle-like) *neck* connecting two mesas. Our word "gap" does not accurately define it.—E. L. H.

The adobe pueblo of *Abèshu'u* (chokecherry end) was situated on the lower mesa three hundred feet above the Chama. It is just south of the present town of Abiquiu. The site is variously known to the Tewa Indians as Abechiu, Josege, and Muké. This may be owing to the fact that there have been several distinct occupations of this village. The ruin is now reduced to low mounds.

On the summit of the second mesa south of the Chama at Abiquiu are ruins of an unusual character. The mesa is crescent-shaped and is about one-half mile wide and a mile and a half long. The top is level and sparsely covered with buffalo grass and a few scrubby pines and piñones. Its general trend is from southwest to northeast. Beginning near the center of the mesa and extending toward the northwest are vestiges of extensive ruins. Only sufficient material remains on the ground to indicate the outlines of the buildings. This consists of cobblestones and small lava blocks, apparently the foundations of ancient walls. The rooms vary from eight to ten feet wide and from fifteen to twenty feet long. In some places they are plainly outlined by the protruding foundation stones, in others barely distinguishable, in some places fading out entirely. They follow the trend of the mesa for over nine hundred yards. One may count the outline of rooms to the number of many hundreds. On my first reconnaissance of the place I estimated that upward of two thousand rooms were plainly traceable. It was in connection with this site that I used the term "pre-Pueblo ruins" for the first time, thereby contributing my share to the subsequent confusion of archaeological nomenclature in the Southwest.

*Tsiping* (flaking stone mountain—Pedernal Peak) is a large ruined pueblo and cliff village on a small detached mesa between the Cañones and Polvadera Creek, four miles south of the Chama River and about fourteen miles from Abiquiu. The site was probably selected for its defensible character, the pueblo being situated some eight hundred feet above the level of the creek, and its walls built flush with the edge of the precipice. The Pedernal Peak from which the village takes its name rises on the opposite side of the canyon about two miles to the southwest. The ruin is accessible by a trail which winds up from the Polvadera and reaches the top of the mesa at its south end, passing thence through two fortified gaps before the pueblo is reached. The site was impregnable against any attack possible in primitive warfare. The commanding position was at the gateway to the Tewa country east of the mountains and, according to tradition, it was the duty of this community to block the raids of enemies from the northwest. The pueblo was built of stone and was three stories high—in places probably four. Portions of second story walls are still standing and many timbers are well preserved. The remains of fifteen kivas, mostly circular, are still traceable in and about the ruins. These were nearly, if not quite, subterranean, having been excavated in the rock surface on which the pueblo stands. The cliff dwellings in the east face of the mesa are of the excavated type and appear to have been used for burial places as well as for dwellings.

Passing now to the ruins in the valley north of the Chama, not on the plateau but belonging with the Pajaritan culture, the first to be noticed is *Yunge* (down at the mocking bird place) or Yuque-yunque of early writers, situated in the delta formed by the conflux of the Chama and the Rio Grande. The site is now occupied by the village of Chamita, of especial interest as the first white settlement in New Mexico, which was founded by Oñate in 1598, and remained the capital for upward of ten years prior to the establishment of Santa Fe. The ruin consists of one irregular quadrangle with large openings on the northwest and southeast. If there were other buildings than the two large structures surrounding the quadrangle, they have been entirely obliterated. This might have occurred, as the site is completely surrounded by cultivated fields. The mounds are well enough preserved to show the form of the pueblo. It was constructed of adobe with considerable use of rubble and small boulders laid in mortar.

The first tributary on the north as one ascends the Chama is the Ojo Caliente. This valley was the home of a number of extensive communities of the Pajaritan breed, or early Tewa. On a hill, about 140 feet above the hot springs which give name to the valley and to the modern town with its bath houses, is the large ruined town of *Posi* (moss-green). It is the largest in the valley. The walls are of adobe, in which are found numerous slabs of stone. Thirteen circular kivas are to be seen in connection with this ruin. It was first described by William H. Holmes.

*Hungpobi* (flower of the one-seeded juniper), sometimes called Homayo or Hupobi, is a large, compactly built pueblo ruin on a promontory on the west side of the Ojo Caliente, about one and a half miles above Posi. The walls are of adobe. There are seven kivas in and about the village. These vary from thirty to fifty feet in diameter and are of circular form. The pueblo was well situated for defense, as it can be readily approached from the west side only. It consisted of one main plaza or court which appears to have been completely closed. Attached to this on the east are two sections which partially inclose a smaller court. Three detached houses stand at a little distance from the main quadrangle.

On a low mesa on the east bank of the creek, just opposite from Hungpobi, is the ruin of *Howiri* (gray point). Here is found one hollow quadrangle, closed except at one corner; another smaller one inclosed by three detached buildings; and two independent sections. The main quadrangle has a perimeter of approximately 1,350 feet. The width of the sections making up the village varies from twenty-five to fifty feet; the number of rooms is indefinite. There are remains of ten circular kivas, ranging from thirty-five to fifty feet in diameter.

Passing up the Chama on the north side, one comes to another tributary, El Rito. In its valley, about five miles below the village of that name, are the ruins of *Sapawe,* now reduced to low rounded mounds. There is a little woodwork still to be seen in the debris of the buildings. Six circular kivas are visible. The village consists of one principal structure forming two incomplete rectangles, and ten detached buildings so disposed as to form a number of smaller courts.

I have here described only the more conspicuous ruins of the northern extension of the Pajarito area. A complete survey would disclose a great number of less conspicuous sites. In the wild, rugged region to the south of this group of ancient settlements there are comparatively few ruins until one reaches the Santa Clara Valley, which gives into the Rio Grande just south of the modern town of Española. Here begins the section that formed the heart of ancient Tewa land. It was visited and briefly described by Stevenson, Powell, and Bandelier in the early 1880's. I commenced here in 1896, kept at it sporadically for nearly ten years, and, after that, continued with classes from time to time until quite recently. My excavations will be described in a later section. The purpose just here is to put down the results of the early mapping which was undertaken for the purpose of getting a picture of the distribution of population in the ancient period. This discussion will begin with the northernmost of the ruins and proceed to the south.

*Shupinna* (narrow point), formerly recorded as Shufinné, is a small pueblo ruin with an accompanying cliff village, situated on a high mesa which rises abruptly above the plateau on the north side of Santa Clara Canyon, about ten miles west of Santa Clara village. The site is a most picturesque one, visible in some directions from a distance of twenty-five miles. The pueblo was rather inferior in construction and is reduced to low mounds. The cliff dwellings are quite generally broken down. An unusual feature of these is the great thickness of the front walls. In some cases, the doorway was cut into the cliff to a depth of four feet before the excavation of the room began. Porches were built in front of the dwellings. The interior rooms are rather crude and usually without smoke vent. Only a small amount of plastering was used.

The pueblo stood back a few yards from the rim of the mesa. It formed a quadrangle seventy-five by ninety feet. But little wall remains standing. However, the outlines may be plainly traced. The rooms average eight by nine feet. The amount of debris is small, indicating that the pueblo was only one story high. Tufa blocks, rudely dressed, were used as building stones. There are remains of one circular kiva approximately twenty feet in diameter within the quadrangle, and another sixteen feet in diameter a few yards from the southeast corner of the building. There are traces of a small reservoir a few yards to the east. The summit of the mesa is an irregular table with diameter of 150 by 240 yards. It bears a few scrubby trees. A defensive wall, the remains of which may be seen a few yards north of the pueblo, extended along the north side. Only a little pottery was found at this site. It conforms to that found at Puyé. The little village is prehistoric.

*Puyé* (where the cottontail rabbits assemble) was a settlement consisting of a large pueblo on the summit of the mesa and an extensive group of cliff villages. The pueblo was a huge quadrangular structure, the most compact and regular of all the large towns. There was one main entrance to the quadrangle near the southeastern corner, and a narrower opening at the southwest. Round kivas, mostly underground, are found both inside and outside of the court. The cliff villages at Puyé were very extensive. The mesa is a mile and a quarter in length and a large portion of the south face is honeycombed with dwellings. A ledge midway up the face of the cliff divides it into two parts. In some places the lower part contains three levels of dwellings, the bottom series being, in many instances, below the talus. The dwellings above the ledge are more scattered, but are also disposed in three levels. A number of caves of unusual size for this locality evidently served the purpose of kivas for the inhabitants of the cliff villages. The excavations at Puyé will be described in a subsequent section.

*Tsipiwi'i* (gap where the pieces of flaking stone come out of the ground) is a small pueblo ruin of imperfect quadrangular form situated on a low mesa about two miles west and a little south of Puyé. It belongs to the older type of pueblos and was one of several minor villages, including Shupinna, that are said to have been tributary to Puyé. An extensive cliff village, consisting mainly of open-front dwellings, occupies the southern exposure of the mesa on which this ruin is located. The ruin stands at the extreme western end of the mesa a few yards back from the brink. On the north and to the west the mesa slopes gently into the Puyé Valley. The pottery fragments found here and in the cliff dwellings are of the more archaic type, as are also the minor artifacts.

In the second valley south of the great pueblo and cliff village of Puyé is a small pueblo ruin known to the Tewa Indians as *Navahu'u* (arroyo of the cultivatable fields), this being, as they claim, the ancient name of the village. This community was well situated for agriculture, there being a considerable acreage of tillable land nearby —far more than this small population would have utilized. The old trail across the neck of the mesa to the north is worn hip-deep in the rock by the attrition of human feet, showing constant, long-continued use. I infer that here were the fields not only of the people of

Navahu'u, but also of the more populous settlements beyond the great mesa to the north, where tillable land is wanting. The name *Navahu'u* suggests an identity with Navajò, which Fray Alonso de Benavides, in his *Memorial* on New Mexico, published in 1630, applied to that branch of the tribe (Apaches of Navajò) then living to the west of the Rio Grande, beyond the section above mentioned. Speaking of these people Benavides says: "But these of Navajò are very great farmers [*labradores*], for that [is what] 'Navajò' signifies —'great planted fields' [*sementeras grandes*]."

These facts may admit of two interpretations. So far as we know, Benavides was the first to use the name *Navajò* in literature, and he would have been almost certain to have derived it from the Pueblos of New Mexico, among whom he lived as Father Custodian of the province from 1622 to 1629, since the Navaho never so designated themselves. The expression "the Apaches of Navajò" may have been used to designate an intrusive band that had invaded Tewa territory and become intrenched in this particular valley. On the other hand, the Navaho, since the pastoral life of post-Spanish times was not then possible to them, may have been so definitely agriculturists, as Benavides states (although he did not extend his missionary labor to them), and have occupied such areas of cultivated lands, that their habitat, wherever it was, would be known to the Tewa as Navahu'u, "the place of great planted fields."

If the first interpretation is correct, it might be verified by archaeological evidences at the ruin of Navahu'u. It would seem, at any rate, that the Tewa origin of the tribal name Navaho is assured.

*Pininikangwi* (dwarf-corn meal gap) is a pueblo ruin considerably smaller than Navahu'u, situated in the same valley about a mile and a half farther from the mountains. It was built in the form of a quadrangle with a single opening on the east side. There was a kiva in the southeast corner of the court. The village was located on a rounded knoll about one hundred yards south of the arroyo. It was probably one story high. The pottery fragments conform to those of Navahu'u.

The *Chupadero* (sucking place—Spanish) refers to a number of cliff villages grouped within and about the Chupadero Canyon. Here is a great network of gorges affording exceptional facilities for defense. There is no pueblo ruin of any considerable size in this section, and the cliff dwellings, numbering many hundreds, are of a quite temporary character. Many are caves in a well-nigh natural state. All fragments of artifacts found here are of very archaic type.

*Perage* (down at the place of the kangaroo rat) is not on the plateau, but is situated on level ground in the valley, a few rods from the west bank of the Rio Grande and a mile west of the Indian village of San Ildefonso. It is included here because of its relation to the ruins on the plateau which rises in huge escarpments of conglomerate and tufa a half mile to the west. This was the site occupied by certain clans of the Powhoge (San Ildefonso) Indians prior to removal to their present location, which occurred some time before the Spanish invasion. It was the first valley site occupied by them on coming down from the pueblo and cliff villages of the plateau to the west, and illustrates their first efforts in building house walls of adobe. Prior to this time adobe had been used by them simply as plaster. This village consisted of twelve sections, four of which were completely detached, two joined together in one building, and the remaining six connected, forming the nucleus of the village and inclosing two large courts. There are remains of three circular, subterranean kivas in the village. Excavations at the site disclosed no traces of Spanish influence. The pottery shows degeneration in its art; decoration falls into decay. The old symbolism of Otowi is gone and the renaissance which came after removal across the river and which resulted in the splendid artistic developments at modern San Ildefonso is not apparent.

About five miles west of the point where the Rio Grande enters White Rock Canyon are the remains of the prehistoric settlement of Otowi or *Potsuwi'i* (gap where the water sinks). It is situated upon a ridge in a valley that will be described in a later section, deeply secluded in the canyons and among the mesas of the middle Pajaritan region. It consists of a cluster of five houses placed on sloping ground and connected at one end by a wall. These were terraced structures, probably almost a counterpart of the present houses at Taos, though perhaps somewhat smaller and containing fewer stories. No house at Otowi could have been more than four stories high. Altogether the five houses contained an estimated number of 450 rooms on the ground floor. The number of superimposed rooms is a matter of conjecture, but I would estimate it at some 250, thus making a total of near 700 rooms in the pueblo. In every direction are excavated cliff dwellings. For the most part they occur in clusters and in two general levels, i. e., at the top of a long steep slope of the talus and again in the face of a second terrace, higher up and difficult of access.

From one-half mile to a mile above the main pueblo is a cliff village that is unique. Here is a cluster of conical formations of almost white tufa, some of which attain to a height of thirty feet. These are properly called "tent rocks." These are full of caves, both natural and artificial, some of which have been utilized as human habitations. These dwellings are structurally identical with those found in the cliffs. They present the appearance of enormous beehives.

There are ten circular kivas at Otowi, all subterranean and outside of the walls of the buildings, with two exceptions. Kivas within the pueblo walls were unusual in the Pajarito Plateau settlements. They exist in the great ruin at the base of Pedernal Peak, Tsiping, and are also found in the older and smaller houses. A reservoir, which may have supplied water for drinking purposes at times, was placed, as was often the case in both ancient and modern pueblos, so as to receive the drainage from the village.

There is a small pueblo ruin in Otowi Canyon just across the arroyo about three hundred yards south of Otowi pueblo. It is situated on the top of a narrow ridge which runs parallel with the one on which the large ruin stands. The stones of the building are smaller and the construction cruder. The building consists of one solid rectangle with a kiva within the court. Seven other small ruins of clan houses are scattered along the same ridge to the west within a distance of one mile, all apparently belonging to this village and antedating the main Otowi settlement.

About two miles southeast of Otowi is the ruin of *Sankewi'i* (gap of the sharp, round cactus), the most picturesquely situated of any settlement of primitive people that I have seen, with the exception of Tsiping. It is a veritable "sky pueblo." From the summit of

Sankewi'i Mesa one looks upon a stupendous panorama—the Jemez range on the west; on the eastern horizon, a hundred miles of the lofty Santa Fe range; glimpses of the Rio Grande and its fertile valley through a cleft some five miles away, beyond which lies a dreary sand waste; and near at hand in every direction huge yellow volcanic mesas and profound depths of wooded canyons. The site is noticeable for its defensive character and is an exceptionally strong one.

The builders of Sankewi'i kept to the orthodox rectangular plan. The masonry is in no respect different from that of Otowi. There were ten kivas at Sankewi'i—a large number for the population, which probably never exceeded three hundred to four hundred people, although this would be considerably increased if we should count the population of the cliff villages in the south face of the mesa. Sankewi'i was a composite pueblo, consisting of four detached houses. The ground plan embraces some two hundred rooms. The sections probably were three stories high. Excavations that have been made at Sankewi'i will be noticed in the account of studies at nearby Otowi. Traditions of Sankewi'i are found at Powhoge. The inhabitants, it is claimed, were Tewa, related to the people of Otowi. They are alleged by some informants to have migrated to the region south of Santa Fe; by others, to have merged with Otowi clans to form the San Ildefonso community.

There is a ruin in Cañon de los Alamos on a high ridge running parallel with the stream on its south side. It is about three-quarters of a mile west of Sankewi'i. The settlement consisted of one rectangular pueblo of considerable size and a number of small clan houses scattered along the ridge to the west for approximately half a mile. It belongs to the older class of ruins. There is also a small pueblo ruin of the older type, located on a lower bench just north of Sankewi'i Mesa, about half a mile south of the Alamo. The walls are entirely reduced.

The village of *Sandia* (watermelon—Spanish) is situated on a high mesa between the Sandia and Bear canyons; it is one of the most commanding sites in Pajarito Park. The pueblo was small, compactly built, forming a complete rectangle. It was probably two stories high. The regularity of the structure was broken by the building of a num-

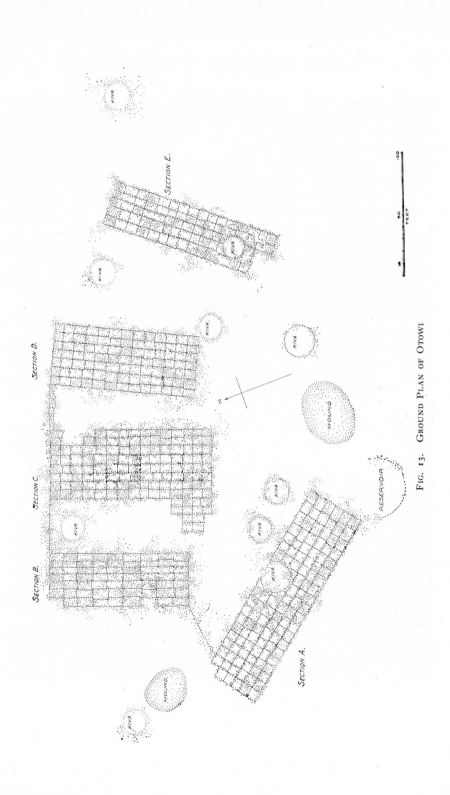

FIG. 13. GROUND PLAN OF OTOWI

Fig. 14.  Rock Trail at Sankewi'i

ber of one-story rooms against the east and north sides. There is one kiva inside the court. In the face of the mesa to the south is a cliff village which includes some of the finest specimens of this type of cliff dwelling within my knowledge. They are unusually well preserved. Many have the plastered doorcasings intact. Some doorways have wooden casings still in place. The rooms were well constructed and conveniently arranged, and, in connection with anterior, open rooms, the evidences of which are plain, must have formed commodious and comfortable homes. This village is in the class with Sankewi'i, with which it was connected by a trail still well preserved and showing long use. The potsherds conform to those of Sankewi'i. All evidences point to this as a contemporary village of possibly two hundred inhabitants. The cemetery is a few yards east of the pueblo. There is a scant growth of piñon and juniper on the mesa top, and it seems probable that some farming was carried on there, though the main fields belonging to the villages were in Bear Canyon, to the south.

Beginning about a mile and a half south of Sankewi'i, the aspect of the country changes. From Pajarito Canyon to Rito de los Frijoles, a distance of perhaps ten miles, the high, abrupt, narrow, tonguelike mesas protruding toward the river, with broad, timbered valleys between, are replaced by one great table land, the Mesa del Pajarito, which, at first sight, appears to be one continuous expanse only partially covered with piñon and juniper. It is, however, deeply cut at intervals by narrow, impassable canyons. Toward the northern limit of this level expanse, about two and a half miles southeast of Sankewi'i, is situated the ruin of *Navawi'i* (pitfall gap). It belongs to the same class and epoch as Otowi and Sankewi'i. It consists of two large buildings some two hundred yards apart, several clan houses on the level mesa nearby, and a cliff village of considerable extent in the face of the low mesa to the south and west. On the narrow neck of a mesa about three hundred yards west of the pueblo, at the convergence of four trails, is a game trap *(nava)* from which the village takes its name. This is one of a number of pitfalls which have been discovered at points in this region where game trails converged. One of the best of these is that at Navawi'i. It was so placed that game driven down the mesa from toward the mountains or up the trail from either of two side canyons could hardly fail to be entrapped. The trap is an excavation in the rock which could have been made only with great difficulty, as the cap of tufa is here quite hard. The pit is bottle-shaped, except that the mouth is oblong. It is fifteen feet deep and about eight feet in diameter at the bottom. The mouth of the pit is about six feet in length by four feet in breadth. This trap has been used in modern times by the San Ildefonso Indians.

*Tsirege* (down at the bird place) is a great ruin situated on a low bluff on the north side of the Pajarito, about six miles west of the Rio Grande. It is on the northern edge of the Mesa del Pajarito, described in connection with Navawi'i. The possibilities for agriculture in this vicinity were considerable during the time when the country was adequately watered. It was the largest pueblo in the Pajarito district, and with the cliff villages clustered about it, the largest aboriginal settlement, ancient or modern, in the Pueblo region, of which I have personal knowledge, with the exception of Zuñi. The ruin shows a ground plan of upward of six hundred rooms. There are ten kivas in and about Tsirege, all of the circular, subterranean type. A defensive wall extended from the southwest corner of the main building to the rim of the cliff 150 feet away. On the face of the cliff below is one of the best petroglyphs to be found in the Southwest. It is a representation of the *Awanyu* or Plumed Serpent, about seven feet in length, etched on the rock by pecking with a stone implement (Fig. 18).

The cliff villages extend along the cliff for three-quarters of a mile. Tsirege is said to have been the last of the villages of Pajarito Park to be abandoned. A limited supply of water can still be obtained at almost any season at the spring in the arroyo a quarter of a mile away, and during wet seasons the Pajarito carries a little water past this point. The remains of a small reservoir are to be seen on the mesa top a few yards north of the main ruin.

There is a small ruin consisting of a single quadrangle situated about three miles west of Tsirege, just south of the abandoned Buckman sawmill road. It belongs to the older class and presents no features of especial interest. A short distance to the west is a game pit similar to the one at Navawi'i.

In the midst of a beautiful open park, three miles southeast of the abandoned sawmill, is a ruin consisting of three compact con-

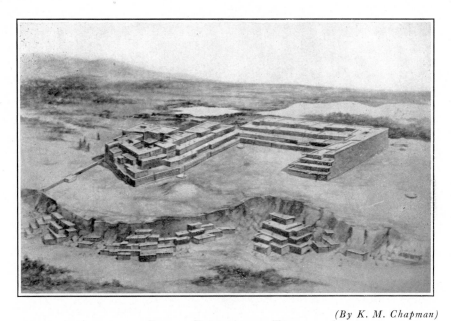

(By K. M. Chapman)

FIG. 15.   RESTORATION OF TSIREGE

FIG. 16.   A SECTION OF THE COMMUNITY HOUSE, PUYÉ—AFTER EXCAVATION

FIG. 17. THE UNIVERSE, JEMEZ KIVA PAINTING

FIG. 18. PETROGLYPH OF AWANYU (PLUMED SERPENT) AT TSIREGE

nected rectangles. No walls are visible above the debris, but on clearing away the loose stone, well preserved plastered walls eight feet in height are disclosed. Numerous small clan houses are scattered about nearby. A few yards to the east is the hollow of a kiva in which a large pine tree is growing. Not far from this ruin are the remains of a circular inclosure built of blocks of tufa set on edge —doubtless an ancient shrine. Less than a mile west, on a high point at the confluence of two very deep gorges, is the best-preserved ruin in this region. The walls stand in places eight feet above the debris. Great pine trees are growing within the rooms. There is evidence that these mesas have been forested since the abandonment of the pueblos. This ruin is almost inaccessible except from the west. It is not less than eight hundred feet above the waters of the Rito del Bravo which it overlooks. The ground plan is very irregular.

In a wooded park just south of the Rito del Bravo and a mile north of Rito de los Frijoles is a small pueblo ruin. It presents no features of particular interest. Nearby are many small clan houses. One may ride for some miles along this mesa and never be out of sight .of ruins of this class.

There is one more large ruin on the mesa between Tsirege and the Rito de los Frijoles. It consists of one compact rectangle. The debris of fallen walls is perhaps eight feet high. A large inclosure walled with stone surrounds the southern and eastern sides of the pueblo. This site overlooks the deep gorge of the Bravo to the north, and a few rods south is another deep canyon. The site is approached by an ancient trail from the west.

It will be interesting at this point to read Adolph Bandelier's account of ruins in the region above described, written almost a quarter of a century earlier than my description. This is to be found in his "Final Report of Investigations Among the Indians of the Southwestern United States," Part II, page 78 ff., *Papers* of the Archaeological Institute of America. It begins with Perage, sometimes called old San Ildefonso, and is quoted as follows:

A little above San Ildefonso stands quite an extensive ruin, through one angle of which the track of the Texas, Santa Fé and Northern Railroad is carried. Pe-ra-ge, as the Indians of San Ildefonso call it, lies not far from the river, on the first terrace of the bluffs. The pueblo was built of rubble and stones, and consisted of several apparently connected quadrangles. It is, therefore, of the type of Se-pä-ue and Abe-chiu, but not as large as the former. The Tehuas of San Ildefonso state that it was inhabited by their ancestors before the coming of the Spaniards, and that they removed thence to the east bank of the Rio Grande. This change of location occurred previous to the sixteenth century. We have, therefore, in this tale about Pe-ra-ge a fragment of the ancient history of San Ildefonso, just as the lore about Chamita affords a glimpse into the past of San Juan, and the tales concerning Pu-yé and vicinity throw light upon that of the Santa Clara tribe.

The country west of the Rio Grande, between Pe-ra-ge in the north and the vicinity of the Rito de los Frijoles in the south, is wild, with deep cañones traversing it like gashes cut parallel to each other from west to east. They are mostly several hundred feet in depth, and in places approaching a thousand. On the northern walls, facing the south or east, caves, usually much ruined, are met with in almost every one of them. There are also several pueblo ruins on the mesas, about which I have only learned from the Indians that they were Tehua villages, and that their construction, occupation, and abandonment antedates perhaps by many centuries the times of Spanish colonization. The Tehua names for these ruins are, respectively, Tzi-re-ge, Sä-ke-yu, and Po-tzu-ye.

Almost opposite San Ildefonso begins the deep and picturesque cleft through which the Rio Grande has forced its way. It is called "Cañon Blanco," "Cañon del Norte," or "White Rock Cañon." Towering masses of lava, basalt, and trap form its eastern walls; while on the west those formations are capped, a short distance from the river, by soft pumice and tufa. As far as I could ascertain, the last two pueblos mentioned lie near the line where the two formations touch each other. Tzi-re-ge stands on a higher level, and is built of pumice and volcanic tufa. It is also called "Pajaro Pinto," from a large stone, a natural concretion, found there, slightly resembling the shape of a bird. The plateau on which this ruin is situated slopes towards the east, and is of inconsiderable height. Its southern side is abrupt, and numerous cave dwellings have been excavated in it. Southeast of the ruin in a bottom lies a spring, with forests all around, though not immediately adjacent to the ruin. Tzi-re-ge was quite large, and comprised several quadrangles, after the manner of the northern Tehua pueblos, but I was not able to make measurements of it. I have seen considerable pottery from it, chiefly black ware, decorated with indented rims, and other simple plastic ornamentation. In a straight line Tzi-re-ge lies seven miles from San Ildefonso, and its altitude above the river I estimate at one thousand feet, if not more.

South of Tzi-re-ge, there are caves in the deep Cañada Ancha and other gorges. On the summit of the Mesa del Pajarito I found ruins of small houses with garden plots.

•

The three villages mentioned as Tzirege, Säkeyu, and Potzuye, are Tsirege, Sankewi'i, and Potsuwi'i or Otowi. The pottery, said to come from Tsirege, is not from there. Its origin is doubtful, but probably modern. It is beautiful in form and of excellent texture. It is totally different from any known ancient pottery found in New Mexico. I have never seen a piece of it that could be localized. Large quantities of it were sold by the curio dealers in Santa Fe years ago as prehistoric pottery from the ruins of Pajaro Pinto. The ruin itself is apparently a myth. The stone mentioned did not come from Tsirege and was never used as a fetish. It is merely a geological freak.

Cliff dwellings of all Pajaritan types are abundant in the region here described. Many of these are in an almost perfect state of preservation. They exhibit the best workmanship that I have seen in this kind of cliff house architecture. This is displayed in the masonry, where any is used, in the shaping of interiors, in the plastering of walls and floors, and in wall painting. In some of the rooms dados are executed in tasteful patterns of yellow and two shades of red. The remains of the best representatives of pueblo-like cliff dwellings built against vertical cliffs and advancing out in several terraces over the talus are here to be seen. An account of our excavations is given in a later section.

When we descend the southern rim of Mesa del Pajarito into the Rito de los Frijoles, we enter the ancient Keres land. Here seems to have been a sharply defined frontier between the communities of Tewa and Keres stocks. From here south to Cañon de Cochiti, the country again assumes the character of that between the Santa Clara and Pajarito canyons. The potreros reach stupendous heights, and the canyons correspondingly great depths. A knowledge of Indian trails is all that will enable one to explore this labyrinth.

In the narrow flood plain of the Rito, on the north side of that brave little stream which still carries on to the Rio Grande, is the main pueblo ruin, which takes its name, *Tyúonyi* (more correctly written Tyó'onye), from that by which the valley is known to the Pueblo Indians, and which designates it as a meeting place or frontier. It is sometimes spoken of as a round pueblo, but is actually an irregular polygon—a single house structure which could have sheltered several hundred people. There are three circular kivas within the court. The building was terraced up from one to four stories.

There are two other ruins of smaller size, one nearly a mile farther down the canyon, having connected with it a kiva and an inclosure on the north side which may have been a shrine. A mile or so above the main ruin is a small pueblo; directly across the stream in front of the Ceremonial Cave, an ancient shrine, which is reached by a climb of ladders and ancient trails 150 feet above the waters of the Rito.

Cliff villages extend from the Ceremonial Cave down stream for nearly two miles, all in the northern wall of the canyon. They are similar to those that have been described above at Puyé, Otowi, and other centers. Numerous kivas occur, excavated in the walls and at the top of the talus slope.

About five miles south of Tyúonyi, after crossing the deep Cañada Honda, one comes to the Potrero de las Vacas, toward the eastern end of which there stands a ruined town that is called the pueblo of the *Yápashenye* (sacred inclosure). It is built of tufa blocks and forms an imperfect rectangle. It contains upward of three hundred rooms on the ground floor, with four kivas inside the court and two outside, nearby. The building was terraced up from one to four

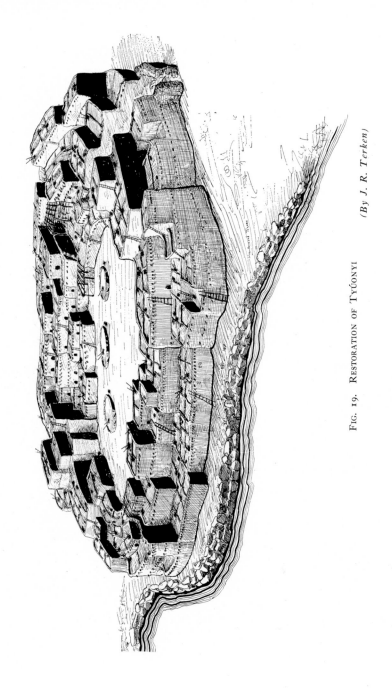

FIG. 19. RESTORATION OF TYÚONYI

(By J. R. Terken)

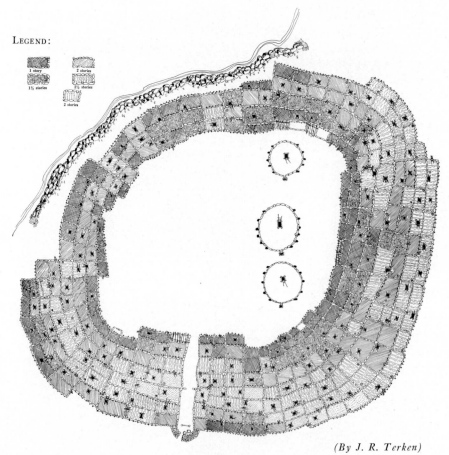

(By J. R. Terken)

FIG. 20.   AERIAL VIEW OF TYÚONYI RESTORED

stories. There is a small reservoir, which was scooped out of the tufa cap, a short distance southeast of the ruin. This village might have accommodated from four to five hundred people.

The name of the above ruin, Yápashenye, is derived from the shrine of the Stone Lions a short distance from the ruin. This was the most important hunting shrine in the entire Pueblo region. Until very recent times it has been visited by Indians from as far away as Zuñi. The two animal figures, representing the mountain lion of the region, are carved in high relief upon a native tufa boulder. They lie crouching side by side with tails extended, the heads pointing to the east. They have been much mutilated by vandals, but are still impressive in appearance. The bodies are about four feet in length; the extended tails, about two feet. There is an inclosure made of slabs of volcanic rock surrounding the figures in the form of an irregular pentagon. It is about seventy feet in circumference and has an opening on the southeast, a little over three feet in width, which forms a walled approach extending about twenty feet from the wall. Indians are still reluctant to show this shrine to white people. They invariably leave it with a brief prayer meal ceremony. Casts of these fetishes were made by Professor Frederick Starr. They may be seen in Walker Museum, Chicago University.

A mile or two south of this group of ruins we come into the Cañada de la Cuesta Colorada. In the north wall of this shallow canyon, about two miles in an air line from the shrine of the Stone Lions, is La Cueva Pintada, the Painted Cave. It somewhat resembles the Ceremonial Cave in the Rito, but is smaller and less regular in form. It is between fifty and sixty feet above the talus slope, and derives its name from the pictographs upon its inner walls. Here are paintings in black, red, and white, displaying many of the well known Pueblo Indian symbols, such as clouds, lightning, sun, shields, and masked dancers. The cave is rather difficult of access; it is not furnished with ladders, and must be reached by way of the ancient trails. There are numerous dwellings in the cliff walls on both sides of the Painted Cave. Some are built in two levels. All are in a very ruinous condition.

At the foot of the range known as Sierra San Miguel is the ruined pueblo of *Há'atse* (earth, world). It consists of five buildings arranged around a square, and could hardly have accommodated more than two or three hundred people. Nearby are two kivas. At a short distance southeast is an artificial reservoir.

On a neighboring mesa known as the Potrero de los Idolos is another shrine of stone lions. The figures were nearly twice as large as those of the Potrero de las Vacas, but artistically inferior. They have been almost destroyed by vandals. There remains about them a ruined stone inclosure made of tufa slabs.

The ruins of *Koapa* (canyon, northwest canyon) lie about a mile and a half down the valley, below an abandoned settlement, about midway between the Potrero de los Idolos and a mesa known as Potrero Viejo. They are on a low bluff between dry arroyos, and are almost obliterated. Remains of half a dozen circular kivas are still to be seen. The village was constructed of tufa, rubble, and adobe.

On Potrero Viejo is an important ruin known as old Cochiti, or *Kótyete*. It is reputed to be the last site of the Cochiti Indians before moving to their present location in the Rio Grande Valley. It was admirably situated for defense, being well supplied with wood, tillable soil nearby, and natural reservoirs for water. It is the largest ruin in this section, and its modern appearance would seem to bear out the tradition of the Cochiti Indians. It seems more than likely that the largest pueblo of this group was built after the Pueblo Rebellion of 1680. If so, it is the one that was abandoned in 1694.

Bandelier was the pioneer explorer and archaeologist of this section. In much of his work he was accompanied by Lummis, whose writings were the first to make the region well known to general readers. Everyone should read Bandelier's description of El Rito de los Frijoles, written in the early 1880's, and first appearing in his ethnological novel, *The Delight Makers*. It can never be equaled, for the modern "improvements" in the incomparable Rito are irreparable. The traditions of Cochiti as related to Lummis by Keres traditionists of fifty years ago, when Pueblo lore was far more reliable than now, can never be superseded. Accordingly, the following extract from "The Wanderings of Cochiti," in *The Land of Poco Tiempo,* is herewith presented by permission of the publishers, Charles Scribner's Sons:

Of that unique racial chess-playing of the Pueblos, whereof the board was half the size of Europe and the chessmen were stone cities, there is one foremost example—the Quéres [Keres] pueblo of Cochití. Other towns may very possibly have moved more (and we know of several movings of each one); but of it we have the clearest and fullest itinerary—a record of eight distinct consecutive moves, beginning many centuries before history, and ending with the Spanish reconquest in 1694. . . .

. . . . . . . . . .

The Tyú-on-yi, the first known home of Cochití, is one of the unique beauties of the Southwest. As a cañon, it is but five or six miles long, and at the widest a quarter of a mile across. Its extreme depth does not exceed two thousand feet. There are scores of greater canyons in this neglected land; but there is only one Tyú-on-yi . . . It was a large town for the prehistoric United States—a town of fifteen hundred to two thousand souls. . . . The line of artificial cave-rooms is a couple of miles long, and in tiers of one, two, and three stories. . . .

. . . . . . . . . .

So exceptionally complete are the links in a story which may very well go far back of William the Conqueror, that we even have legendary hints of the subdivisions of this immemorial village; and in a cave-room of the cluster which has suffered most from the erosion of the cliff, I once stumbled upon gentle José Hilario Montoya, the [later] Governor of the new Cochití, wrapped in his blanket and in reverie. He had stolen away from us, to dream an hour in the specific house that was of his own first grandfathers.

We have no means of knowing just how long the strange white town of the Rito has been deserted, but it has been many, many centuries; for its hunted people built successive towns, and farmed and fought and had a history in each of six later homes before the written history of America began. Though eternally harassed by the Navajos, the Tyú-on-yi held its own, we are told, until destroyed by its own brethren. . . .

The survivors of the final catastrophe abandoned their ruined town in the Rito, and moving a day's march to the south, established themselves upon the table-top of the great Potrero de las Vacas. They were now seven or eight miles west of the chasm of the Rio Grande, and on the summit of the tongue-plateau between two of its principal side-cañons. They were a mile from water—the sparkling brooklet which flows past the Cueva Pintada—and therefore from their farms. But feeling this inconvenience little so long as it gave safety, they reared among the contorted junipers a new town—essentially unlike the quaint combination-pueblo of the Rito, but like to a more common pattern. It was the typical rectangular stone box of continuous houses, all facing in. Here on the grim mesa, amid a wilderness of appalling solitude, they worried out the tufa blocks, and builded their fortress-city, and fended off the prowling Navajo, and fought to water and home again, and slept with an arrow on the string. How many genera-tions of bronze babies frolicked in this lap of danger; and rose to arrowy youth that loved between sieges; and to gray-heads that watched and counselled; and to still clay that cuddled to the long sleep in rooms thenceforth sealed forever, there is no reckoning—nor when was the red foray, whereof their legends tell, of an unknown tribe which finished the town of the Mesa of the Cows. But when the decimated Quéres left that noble site, they left, besides their fallen home, a monument of surpassing interest. . . . The only examples of life-size carvings, or of any *alto relievo,* ever found in the enormous range of the Pueblos, are the four astonishing figures which were, and are, the homotypes of the chase-gods of wandering Cochití.

. . . . . . . . . . . .

. . . It was reserved for the Cochiteños to invent and realize a life-size fetich—therefore, one nearer the actual divinity symbolized, and more powerful. And from that far, forgotten day to this incon-gruous one, the stone lions of Cochití have never lost their potency. Worshipped continually for longer ages than Saxon history can call its own, they are worshipped still. No important hunt would even now be undertaken by the trustful folk of Cochití without first repair-ing to the stone pumas, to anoint their stolid heads with face-paint and the sacred meal, and to breathe their breath of power.

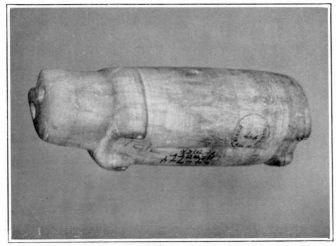

FIG. 22. MOUNTAIN LION FETISH OF
ALABASTER FROM TSIREGE

FIG. 21. THE STONE LIONS OF COCHITI

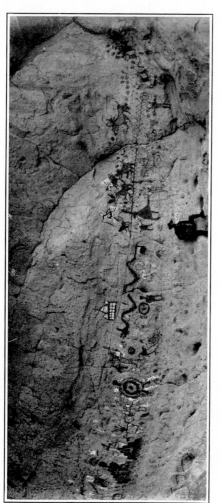

Fig. 23. Detail of Paintings in La Cueva Pintada, Colorado Canyon

Fig. 24. Talus Unit A, Northern Cliff, Tyúonyi

But now the town of the lions had fallen, and a second migration was imperative. In this new move to checkmate the tireless aggressor, the Cochiteños took a sort of "knight's leap." They dropped fifteen hundred feet from the mesa's top to the cañon, and thence at a right angle three miles down the brook, namely, to the Cueva Pintada. The site of this, their third known town, which they called Tsé-ki-a-tán-yi, was far ahead, in safety and in picturesqueness, of the second. In both these qualities it somewhat recalls the peerless Rito. The cañon is wider and not so deep, but of similar formation, and similarly wooded and watered. As always, the wanderers chose its noblest point. There the northern cliff of white pumice is five hundred feet high, and in its face is a great natural cave like a basin set on edge, fifty feet above the ground. Along the foot of this fine cliff they hewed out their cave-rooms and built their tufa masonry, and in the arch of the great natural cave itself they hollowed other chambers, attainable only by dizzy toeholes in the sheer rock. The Painted Cave seems to have had some of the uses of a shrine, and along the crescent of its inner wall may still be traced prehistoric pictographs (along with more modern ones) done in the red ochre which abounds farther up the cañon. There are figures of the Kö-sha-re, the delight-makers, and of the sacred snake whose cult—once universal among the Pueblos—has still such astounding survival at Moqui; and of the round, bright house of the Sun-Father and of the morning and evening stars, and many other precious symbols.

At last the turn of Tsé-ki-a-tán-yi came too, and there was a day when they who had burrowed in its gray cliffs must bid it farewell. The cause of this migration is not certain. It may have been moral or military; omen of divine displeasure, or merely an overdose of Navajo—for the whole region was ceaselessly harried by this most powerful race of desert pirates. At all events, the beset Quéres had finally to abandon their third town and seek a fourth. This time they moved south a short march and built Rătya, whose ruins are now known as San Miguel. Here again they dwelt and suffered and made history; and from here again they were at last compelled, by supernatural or hostile pressure, to move on. Their fifth stone town they built in the Cañada de Cochití, twelve miles northwest from the present pueblo, and named it Cuá-pa. There was, and is, a lovely thread of a valley, just widening from the dark jaws of the cañon which splits the Potrero Viejo from its giant brother to the north.

Half-way back on the trail to the Cueva, atop the almost inaccessible Potrero de los Idolos, Bandelier—who was also the discoverer of the Rito, the Cueva Pintada, and the Potrero de las Vacas with its wonderful images—found two other stone cougars. They are life-size, but of different design from those of the northern *potrero;* less weathered, and evidently of later, though still prehistoric, origin. They, also, were carved in high relief from the bedrock with obsidian knives; they, likewise, faced south and were surrounded by a fence of tufa slabs. But they have not been as undisturbed. . . .

Driven in time from the Cañada, as they had been driven from four previous towns, the Quéres climbed the seven-hundred-foot cliffs of the Potrero Viejo, which overhangs the Cañada. Here was their sixth town—Há-nut Cochití, or Cochití Above—and their most impregnable. Nowhere save by the three vertiginous trails is it possible to scale that aërial fortress; and we may presume that here at last they were able to defy their savage neighbors. With time, however, the difficulties of farming and watering at such long range seem to have induced them to remove to the banks of the Rio Grande, just where it emerges from its grewsome gorge to the widening vales of Peña Blanca. Here they raised their seventh pueblo, this time largely of adobe; and here they were when the history of America began. There is nothing to indicate that the Cochití which has been known now for three hundred and fifty years, has been longer occupied than was any one of the six towns which preceded it; though of course the presumption is that it has. Here the Spanish world-openers found the town, and here the Cochiteños voluntarily became vassals of Spain and were baptized into the church of the new God. Here, too, nearly a century and a half later, they helped to brew that deadliest insurrection which ever broke on United States soil; and on that red August 10, 1680, their warriors were of the swarthy avalanche that befell the undreaming Spaniards. They had a hand in the slaying of the three priests of their parish, who were stationed at Santo Domingo; and were among the leading spirits of all those bloody years of the Pueblo rebellion.

The only fight in which they are known to have figured largely, however, was at the reconquest. When Diego de Vargas, the *Reconquistador,* came, they abandoned Cochití and went back to their long-ruined citadel on the Potrero Viejo. This seventh town-moving did not save them; for in the spring of 1694 Vargas and his "army" of one hundred and fifty men stormed that aboriginal Gibraltar. In the desperate but short assault only twenty-one Indians were slain. Indeed, the decimation of the Cochiteños was due not at all to the Spaniards, but to their one-sided wars with the Navajos and with other Pueblos; to epidemics, and to social centrifuge—for the legendary hints are strong that not only Cochití but *all* the Quéres pueblos originated in the Tyú-on-yi. If this be true, the six present Quéres pueblos to the south and west of Cochití, with their prehistoric predecessors—for each had its town-movings—were doubtless founded by early rovers from the Rito, until all were gone from the first nest save the later wanderers whom we have been following.

After the reconquest the Cochiteños abandoned their second town on the Potrero Viejo, and moving for the eighth time, returned to their present pueblo, where they have ever since remained. It is seldom that any of them visit the old homes. Only when there is to be a ceremonial hunt do they trudge away to their ancient Chase-Fetiches to drink the mighty breath of Mokeitcha. The trails are so fearfully rough that one can go all the way to the Rito much sooner afoot than on even the tireless Indian pony; and they are lonely now, and grown very dim. The ankle-deep wee crystals of the potrero-tops outsparkle the Valley of the Rocs, unscuffled by passing feet. The wild turkey drinks unscared from the Rito de los Frijoles, and blinks at its sun-bewildered walls. The tawny puma purrs in the white light beside his gray stone prototypes on the Potrero de las Vacas or the Potrero de los Idolos. And Cochití, at rest at last, dreams on its sunward gravel bank along the swirling Rio Grande, and tills its happy fields, and goes to its Christian mass, and dances unto the Trues, and forgets that ever there was war and wandering.

•

We have now, in this survey, reached the southern limit of ancient Pajaritan culture. All the ruins north of El Rito de los

Frijoles seem to be ancient Tewa. Those from the Rito south to old Cochiti are the oldest Keres settlements that are known to us as such. It appears fairly certain that in this section the early Keres had their initial development, and that from here their dispersion to the Rio Grande Valley took place. There are the living Keres towns, and to the west are the modern Acoma and Laguna villages. Between the two groups lie the little-known ruins of the Rio Puerco Valley which in all probability are of Keres origin.

# PART THREE

# PICK, TROWEL, AND SPADE

## I. The Pajaritan Builders: Classification of Ruins, Excavation

THE RANGE of building activity among the ancient Pajaritans was small as compared with that of peoples west of the Continental Divide. We miss the double- and triple-walled towers of the San Juan drainage, the "great sanctuaries" of Chaco Canyon and beautifully finished masonry of the Chaqueños. Their buildings were mainly for residential purposes, with such kivas as were necessary in the religious and governmental life. We have then to deal mainly with buildings devoted to house life. These were of two sorts, cliff dwellings and pueblos. By the first I mean those ancient dwellings of sedentary Indians that are wholly or in part embraced within cliffs, built against cliffs, or situated on ledges under overhanging cliffs. They are both single- and multiple-chambered, both isolated and communal. By the second term I mean the community houses of the Pueblo Indians that are situated on mesas or in valleys, independent of support from natural rock walls. They are both ancient and modern, and are always multiple-chambered.

Popular nomenclature long ago settled upon the terms *cliff dwelling* and *pueblo*. They are exact enough for all practical purposes. Geological environment gave rise to the first, and social organization to the second term. There are no structural differences on which to separate them. Geological environment gives name to the cliff dwelling. A pueblo would be a cliff dwelling if it were situated against or under a cliff. If away from the cliff environment it remains a pueblo. "A fog is a cloud in which you are. A cloud is a fog in which you are not." Dr. Fewkes made the fundamental difference one of *dependence*

63

on or *independence* of natural rock walls, and the distinction seems quite adequate.

The term *pueblo* is applied to a single structure or to a cluster of such structures. There is but one kind of pueblo—it is a cluster of rooms or cells. There are numerous variations of extension or arrangement, but not of structure. The cells may be placed irregularly or they may follow a definite alignment of common wall. They may be arranged in one story or with superimposed stories. The orthodox form of the Rio Grande pueblo is an arrangement of four sections or of four separate houses inclosing or nearly inclosing a quadrangle. There is a general tendency to form quadrangles, but most of them are incomplete and there are many more aberrant than orthodox arrangements. Two elements enter into the morphology of the pueblo cluster. New buildings or large sectional additions are occasioned usually by the arrival of new clans. New cells in clusters of two or more are added to the side, front, back, or top of the maternal residence as new marital alliances are contracted. Pueblo daughters do not "marry off" as ours do; rather they "marry on," as I used to hear said in the rural districts by men whose sons-in-law came to live at the daughters' ancestral home. The new family is annexed to the maternal clan, and unless prevented by unusual conditions, the daughter will build her home adjoining that of her mother. It might almost be stated as a law of growth for Pueblo houses that development in any direction or quarter is in proportion to the number of daughters born there, and that decay or abandonment of rooms proceeds in an inverse ratio to the number of daughters. I am aware that certain influences sometimes annul this natural tendency. Thus the gradual accretion of new rooms which is occasioned by new marriages tends to irregularity of arrangement with reference to the general ground plan, while large additions occasioned by the arrival of considerable numbers at one time tend to symmetrical growth. In the district under consideration every arrangement possible to rectangular blocks or cells is represented by numerous examples.

The many single-chambered structures scattered over the formerly arable valleys and mesas are not to be regarded as pueblos; they were used as camps or lookouts, as similar structures today are used in summer by the Tewa. The building had only a partial wall. The masonry was usually carried to a height of three or four feet. There was an open space above the half-wall, closed with brush as occasion demanded, and the structure was surmounted by a brush roof. It is a survival of the ancient pit house.

In considering the domiciles of the cliffs I cannot accept the classification of my predecessors. The term *cliff dwelling* applies so perfectly to all domiciles of the cliff environment and is so firmly established by popular usage that I cannot bring myself to use the classification into cave dwellings, cavate lodges, and *true* cliff dwellings. They are all equally true cliff dwellings. I prefer to drop the term "cave dwelling" from the nomenclature of the Southwest, restricting it to the widely different culture of the so-called "cave men," or dwellers in natural caves, and then to use but the one term to designate all cliff homes. The term so used embraces a wide range of structures which shade insensibly from one to another. This gradation is shown in the accompanying series of photographs from Pajarito Plateau. It will be seen that there are certain differences, bridged over in various ways but nevertheless affording a valid basis for separation, as follows:

A—*Open front dwellings:* These are usually, but not always, single-chambered; not in strongly defensive sites; originally shaped by wind erosion but enlarged and modified by excavation, the only industrial process employed in their construction.

B—*Excavated dwellings with closed front:* These have the common characteristic of a front wall either of the natural rock *in situ,* or of masonry. They are usually, though not always, multiple-chambered; wholly artificial; usually in strong defensive sites; floors commonly below the level of the threshold; generally with a crude fireplace beside the doorway; frequently provided with a smoke vent; rooms roughly rectangular and well shaped; floors and walls plastered; dado in red usually around the base of the wall; front walls from a foot to four feet thick. This form displays great advance over A in constructive skill. In A the only industrial process employed was excavation or digging. In the various forms of B a considerable variety of constructive processes is displayed, viz., excavation, masonry, plastering, painting, and carpentry.

Figure 25c shows the simplest form of B; it has a small rectangular doorway without casing. Figure 25d illustrates the introduction of masonry. The doorway is cased in stone laid in adobe mortar. The dwelling is furnished with a smoke vent. These appear to be improvements on a dwelling originally like that shown in Fig. 25c. Figure 25e shows a perfectly preserved casing surrounded with additional and well preserved masonry. Figure 25f illustrates a free use of masonry to replace the entire front wall of natural rock which had fallen away.

Figure 25g illustrates a still more advanced use of masonry; almost the entire front wall is artificial, and the masonry is the best I have seen in this section. The rooms are finely shaped. This was a small natural cavern under an overhanging ledge, excavated into the desired shape and then walled up. It is located in Sandia Canyon. Figure 25h is similar to Fig. 25e. It has a cased doorway and has the new feature of a vestibule excavated from the natural rock. This vestibule was roofed and served the purpose of a room. The back room was furnished with a smoke vent. Figure 25i is a restoration and is, I think, quite true to history. It consists of the excavated room with an external porch which served for living purposes more than did the cave rooms. These porches were built of poles, stone, and brush, the cliff wall furnishing the posterior support for roof and floor beams. They were in general use throughout the district.

C—*Pueblo-like cliff dwellings:* These exhibit every feature of independent pueblos. They are built of stone. Masonry, plastering, and carpentry are involved. They display advance in constructive skill over B, principally in masonry. In their development they were subject to the same laws that governed the growth of independent pueblos. Figure 15 shows this style built against the cliff. Those illustrated were at Tsirege and could be shown only by restoration. The foundation walls were clearly defined. The upper stories were not superimposed upon lower chambers, but rested on the talus. Back of the rooms which abutted against the cliff were excavated rooms used for storage, and, in some cases, as burial crypts.

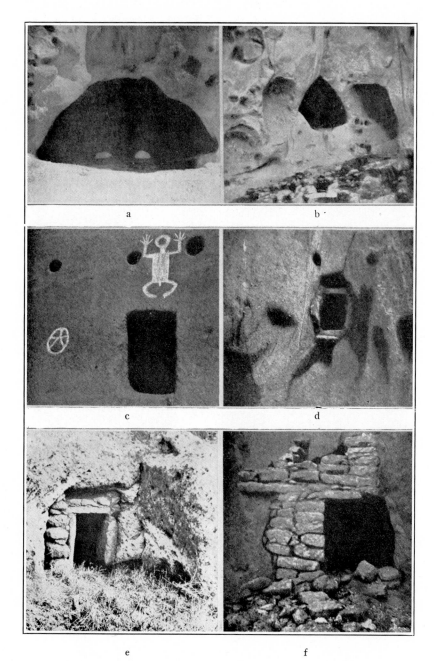

a                 b

c                 d

e                 f

FIG. 25.  TYPICAL CLIFF DWELLINGS OF THE PAJARITO PLATEAU
(Continued on next page)

g                                    h

i

FIG. 25 *(Continued)*.  TYPICAL CLIFF DWELLINGS OF THE PAJARITO PLATEAU

Figure 26 is of Spruce Tree House in Mesa Verde—a so-called *true* cliff dwelling. It is introduced here to complete the series of illustrations of pueblo-like cliff dwellings. There is no example of the community cliff dwelling built on ledges under overhanging cliffs on Pajarito Plateau. A and B include those dwellings usually classed as cavate lodges. C comprises those that are structurally identical with pueblos. The classification, by both methods, of the examples figured is concisely shown as follows:

I. Cliff dwellings: A, Figs. 25a and b; B, Figs. 25c to i; C, Figs. 15 and 26.

II. Pueblos: Fig. 15.

As classified by Dr. Fewkes and others:

I. Cavate dwellings: Fig. 25.

II. Cliff dwellings: Fig. 27.

III. Pueblos: Fig. 15.

While the distribution, construction, and general arrangement of the ruins may be understood by surface exploration, it requires excavation to answer many vital questions in Pueblo archaeology. We shall, therefore, present a non-technical account of our major excavations in the Pajaritan ruins.

The following account will apply to all the large pueblos of Pajarito Plateau. They are all, with one exception, built of roughly shaped blocks of volcanic tufa, averaging about six inches in thickness and eight inches in width. The blocks vary in length from one to four feet. The buildings present no features of construction that are unusual in pueblo architecture. The blocks were laid in adobe mortar. Small stones for chinking were freely used. Inner walls, when protected by debris, are covered with adobe plaster which shows evidence of many successive renewals. Doorways in the interior average about fifteen by forty inches in size, cased with wood, nearly all with stone sills. There are small round windows, usually less than a foot in diameter, near the floor. This feature is found in all the cliff dwellings of the region and suggests a possible function in ventilation. The timbers used were small, rarely exceeding six inches, often not more than four inches in diameter. This is a singular circumstance when we consider that it occurs in an area where large timbers were plentiful and near at hand. In the large pueblos of Chaco Canyon the timbers average much larger, notwithstanding the fact that the Chaco Canyon pueblos are situated in a treeless country. Timbers forty feet long and eighteen inches in diameter have been found in the Chaco ruins.

Another interesting point of comparison between the buildings of these two regions is in their masonry. Much smaller blocks of stone prevail in the Chaco buildings, and they present smoother and more beautiful walls than those of the Pajarito. This does not necessarily point to greater constructive skill, for the natural cleavage of the Chaco sandstone renders dressing almost unnecessary, while the dressing of volcanic tufa of the Pajarito would leave comparatively rough surfaces. The building stone of the Chaco lent itself readily to tasteful arrangement in alternating courses of thick and thin blocks, and also made the unique curved walls of these pueblos possible. The rough tufa blocks of the Pajarito could not easily be worked and set in this way, and they permitted of no decorative effect in arrangement of courses. The difference in material also accounts for the great difference in the preservation of walls. The flat slabs of sandstone of the Chaco fit together quite perfectly, with but little mortar to weather out. The imperfectly flattened surfaces of the Pajarito tufa blocks are readily freed by the weather from the supporting mortar and chinking stones, and collapse of the walls soon follows.

In the Pajarito it is only in exceptional cases that walls remain above the surrounding debris to a height of more than seven or eight feet, while in the Chaco, walls still stand at a height of forty to fifty feet. An evidence that the height of ruined walls bears little relation to the age of ruins is seen in the fact that some of the ruins of the Tyúonyi group are almost leveled to the ground, the convex surfaces of the stone affording no stability to the walls. These buildings were occupied in comparatively recent times.

While engaged in the exploration and mapping of Pajarito Plateau from 1897 to 1902, I made some preliminary excavations at Puyé, Tsirege, Sankewi'i, and nearby small house sites. It was amateur

FIG. 26.   SPRUCE TREE HOUSE, MESA VERDE

FIG. 27.   RECONSTRUCTION OF TALUS UNIT, TYÚONYI

work but served to bring to the attention of the archaeologists of that time a culture of which very little was known. I wish to acknowledge my indebtedness to William H. Holmes, of the United States National Museum; Frederick W. Putnam, of Harvard University; and Frederick Starr, of the University of Chicago, for the encouragement which I received from them. As I brought items concerning what I was doing to their attention from time to time, there came invariably, and with surprising promptness, a word of appreciation, with perhaps a suggestion of something that might add to the value of the work. What a lot of younger archaeologists "take off their hats" to the memory of these inspiring men!

## II. The Excavation of an Ancient Tewa Town: Puyé

In the summer of 1907, work was begun on the ruins of Puyé in coöperation with the Southwest Society of the Archaeological Institute of America. This was the first of the ancient pueblos of the Rio Grande Valley to be systematically excavated, and the second ruin in the United States to be treated with a view to its permanent preservation.

Puyé is one of the most extensive of the ancient towns of the Southwest. It occupies an imposing situation on the Pajarito Plateau, ten miles west of the village of Española and thirty miles northwest of Santa Fe. Since 1880 the place has received some attention in the writings of Powell, Bandelier, Lummis, and myself. Through widely published photographs its general appearance has been well known for some years, and much has been said concerning its history, based upon surface evidence and Tewa story. But it is the spade that must be depended upon to lay bare the irrefutable record.

At first, opposition to the excavation of the ruins was offered by the Indians from the nearest Tewa village, Santa Clara, ten miles away in the Rio Grande Valley, on whose reservation the site is located. The governor, head men, and representatives of the caciques or religious rulers, were met in council and the matter frankly laid before them. It was explained that this was our way of studying the history of the Indian tribes; that we believed that the thoughts and works of their ancestors and of the other peoples with whom they had been in contact constituted a record worthy of being recovered and preserved for all time. Some appeal was made to their sense of gratitude for assistance rendered them in the past in securing from the government a much needed and justly deserved extension of their reservation, and a law releasing them from the payment of taxes on their lands, which at one time had threatened the extinction of the titles to their homes. Bare reference was made to the fact that under the permit of the Department of the Interior we were acting within our rights in making excavations on their reservation, for it was desired to rely mostly upon their own sense of right and wrong. I regret that I am unable to reproduce the speeches of the head men on the subject. They abounded in cogent argument which demanded unequivocal answer. On the whole, their contention was on a high plane, and their deliberations marked by much lofty sentiment. It ended in all objection being withdrawn and most cordial relations established, which were afterward expressed in a perfectly friendly interest in our work.

It is not an exaggeration—just a blunder—to speak of Puyé as a "cliff city." If used, it must be understood that the term does not imply a civic organization comparable to that of our modern municipalities. There were, in the social organization that existed here, some elements of collective order that characterize the civic group which we designate by the term "city." There was regulated community life and definite social obligation. The population was ample to constitute a fair-sized modern town.

Geologically, Puyé is a rock of grayish-yellow tufa, 5,750 feet long, varying in width from ninety to seven hundred feet. It is a fragment of the great tufaceous blanket which once covered the entire Pajarito Plateau to a thickness of from fifty to fifteen hundred feet. This covering of tufa has been completely dissected by ages of water and wind erosion. In the northern part not over 10 per cent of it remains. These fragments appear as a multitude of geological islands, some almost circular, but mostly long potreros extending east and west from the base of the Jemez Mountains towards the Rio Grande. On the south side they present vertical escarpments rising above talus slopes which usually reach almost to the dry arroyos in the valley bottoms. The north side is always less abrupt, presenting only small escarpments and long, gentle slopes to the valley. There is scant soil on the tops of these mesas, and vegetation is limited to grass, juniper and piñon. The valleys are lightly forested with pine of not very ancient growth. The altitude is approximately seven thousand feet above sea level.

The view from the summit of the rock of Puyé is almost beyond compare. A few miles to the west is the Jemez range with its rounded contours and heavily forested slopes. On the eastern horizon one sees a hundred and fifty miles of the Santa Fe range, embracing the highest peaks in New Mexico. The northern extremity of the panorama lies in the state of Colorado, and at the south end, near Albuquerque, is the rounded outline of Sandia Mountain, *Oku piñ,* of Tewa mythology. The great synclinal trough of the Rio Grande extends from north to south between the two ranges. The portion of it here seen formed the bed of a Miocene lake. The great expanse of yellowish-gray Santa Fe marl, which the winds have piled into rounded dunes and trimmed into turreted castles, presents at all times a weird and fantastic appearance. In the immediate foreground to the east one looks down upon the level plateau stretching away to the valley. In the summer and fall this is variegated by masses of yellow flowers, which cover the open parks among the junipers, marking the fields of the ancient inhabitants. Beyond this lie several miles of open grass lands. To the northwest, about a mile and a half, the yellow rock of Shupinna dominates the plain, and to the west and south lie the detached masses which I have spoken of as geological islands. Southeast, some ten miles, the round black bulk of *Tuñjopiñ* (very spotted mountain) rises on the east bank of the Rio Grande. Here is an example of the geologically recent basaltic extrusions which characterize the Rio Grande Valley from this point south through White Rock Canyon. This is the historic Black Mesa, the scene of many stirring events of the early period of Spanish occupation. In Tewa mythology, "Tuñjo" is the sacred fire mountain. Its summit is covered with the remains of semi-subterranean dwellings, and fire shrines are still maintained there by the Indians of San Ildefonso.

Puyé was the principal focus of a population that occupied a number of villages in the northern part of this plateau. There are many small house ruins, containing anywhere from two to fifty rooms each, scattered all over the district. Villages are found on the top of almost every mesa of any size. The large settlements consisted of one to three quadrangular pueblos, one or more small houses nearby, and a village of excavated rooms in the nearest adjacent cliff wall. These have been discussed sufficiently in a previous section.

The settlements described seem to have been rather closely related. The villages were all connected by well worn trails, some of them of unusual depth. One crosses a narrow neck *(wi'i)* of the mesa of Pininikangwi. With the exception of one at Sankewi'i, it is the deepest worn rock trail that I have seen. It seems to have been made entirely by the attrition of human feet, being so situated that its depth could not be augmented by water erosion. The network of trails to be seen over this entire plateau is one of its most interesting archaeological features. The trail is a sharply cut path, usually about eight inches wide, from a few inches to a foot in depth—in some places more. The path narrows but little toward the bottom and is remarkably clean cut (Fig. 14). A large part of the surface of the plateau is rock, devoid of soil, and these paths afford an imperishable record of ages of coming and going.

The Puyé is a fine example of the ancient Pajaritan community. At this place is found everything that is characteristic of the Pajaritan culture—every form of house ruins, typical in construction and placement; sanctuaries, pictographs, implements, utensils, symbolic decoration—all following a well defined order, and conforming in essential particulars to the type of culture to which I gave the name Pajaritan.

The Puyé settlement was made up of two aggregations of dwellings: (1) The great quadrangle on the mesa top, an arrangement of four huge terraced community houses about a court, forming at once an effective fortification and a capacious dwelling—a compact residential fortress that might not inappropriately be called the citadel. (2) The cliff villages, consisting of a succession of dwellings built against and within the wall of the cliff, usually at the level where the

FIG. 28.   AN OTOWI BASKET BURIAL

FIG. 29.   EXAMPLES OF BONEWORK FROM PAJARITAN RUINS

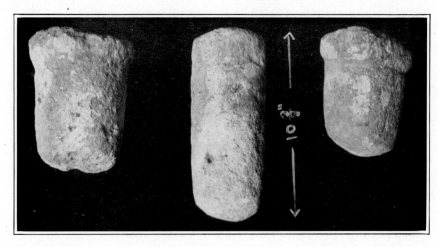

FIG. 31. CEREMONIAL STONES FROM OTOWI

FIG. 30. TYPES OF ARROW STRAIGHTENERS FOUND IN PAJARITAN EXCAVATIONS

talus slope meets the vertical escarpment. The latter will be described first.

An almost continuous succession of dwellings is to be seen along the face of the cliff from one end to the other. The cliff is more than a mile (5,750 feet) in length. We note here three classes of dwellings: (1) Excavated, cave-like rooms, serving as domiciles, without any form of construction in front (Fig. 25a). (2) Excavated rooms with open rooms or porches built on in front (Fig. 25i). (3) Houses of stone, one to three stories high, with corresponding number of terraces, built upon the talus against the cliff. In these groups the excavated chambers now seen in the cliff wall were back rooms of the terraced buildings. Such was the example shown in Fig. 15. An examination of the talus discloses remains of the walls of several villages of considerable extent which were built against the cliff. Figure 32 shows a section of the cliff which was the site of one of these talus pueblos, a building two stories high. A row of holes in the cliff wall shows where the ceiling beams of the second story rested. The walls of first-floor rooms are to be found under the debris where the talus meets the vertical cliff. The ruins of a number of excavated back rooms are to be seen in the wall.

The cliff is broken about midway of its height by a ledge which shelves back a few yards and then meets another vertical wall. On this ledge, and against and within this upper wall, are the remains of another succession of dwellings. These continue for a distance of 2,100 feet. This, added to the line of dwellings on the lower level, gives a continuous extent of house remains about a mile and a half in length. Dwellings of the upper ledge were quite like those below. Here were the simple cave-like houses, the porched chambers, and the terraced house against the cliff, with excavated back rooms. It was possible to step from the house-tops onto the rim rock above. In places retaining walls of stone were built on the front of the ledge. Stairways cut in the face of the rock ascend from the upper ledge to the community house on the summit.

The great community house stands near the edge of the cliff, the southwest corner approaching to within twenty feet of the brink. The huge quadrangular pile of tufa blocks gives, at first, the impression of great regularity of construction, but on close examination the usual irregularities of Pueblo buildings are found. It would require a rectangle approximately 300 by 275 feet to inclose the ruin. No two interior walls are exactly parallel, but the orientation of the building is approximately with the cardinal points. The wall forming the east side of the court is on a due north and south line. The interior court is not a perfect rectangle, the north side measuring 150 feet, south 140, east 158, and west 143 feet.

At the southeast corner is the main entrance to the square, seventeen feet wide at the eastern end, but enlarging to double that width before it opens into the court. A narrow passage thirteen feet wide, not known to exist until excavations began, was cleared at the southwest corner of the court, thus segregating the south house of the quadrangle from the other four sides. It is probable that this latter was a covered passage. Excavation may disclose other entrances to the court.

One subterranean sanctuary, or kiva, is found against the outer wall of the east house, and another, somewhat larger, lies 165 feet northeast of this one. The largest kiva on the mesa top, apparently about thirty-six feet in diameter, lies sixty feet west of the southwest corner of the quadrangle. These kivas were all excavated in the rock, there being almost no covering of soil at this place. Others are found on the ledge of the cliff below, and still others in the talus.

The ruins of an ancient reservoir lie 120 feet west of the pueblo. It is oblong in form and measures about 75 by 130 feet in diameter. The embankment is made of stone and earth, the opening being on the west. It could not have been fed from any living source, and could have been useful only for impounding such surface water as would be conducted to it through the small draw to the west. The potable water for the pueblo must have been derived from what is now the dry arroyo south of the mesa. At one point, a meager amount can still be obtained by opening a spring in the sand, but here, as on all parts of this plateau, a much more plentiful water supply than that now existing would be essential to the maintenance of such large settlements as once existed at Puyé. An evidence of such supply is to be seen in the irrigation canal which may be traced for nearly two miles along

FIG. 32.   PUYÉ MASONRY WITH SMALL ROCK SPALLS

FIG. 33.   REMAINS OF TALUS ROOMS BUILT IN FRONT OF CLIFF

the south side of Puyé arroyo. This ditch heads above the mesa toward the mountain, and must have been used to conduct surface water from mountain gulches to the level fields south and east of the settlements. It is possible that it was constructed during a late occupation of Puyé by the Santa Clara Indians, after their knowledge of irrigation had been augmented by contact with the Spaniards in the Rio Grande Valley.

When it came to excavating the ruin, a line of Indian workmen stationed themselves across the great pile of the fallen building, gathered the loose stones and passed them along by hand to a pile outside of the quadrangle. When loose stones and all that could be freed from the debris by picks were thus disposed of, and the standing walls disclosed, plank runways were laid and shovels and wheelbarrows brought into service. Earth and broken stone filled the rooms to a depth of several feet, and in the removal of this most of the specimens were found. The rooms were usually plastered and well floored. In some cases rooms were found with secondary floors, laid upon a considerable depth of soil and debris, indicating re-occupation after a period of disuse.

For the remaining description of the excavation of Puyé, I utilize the account written by my assistant, Sylvanus G. Morley, on the conclusion of the work in 1909:

The south house at Puyé is the southern member of a large community house, of rectangular ground plan, which encloses a court, nearly an acre in extent. Unlike the other three houses surrounding this central court, the south house stands by itself, there being alleyways at both its eastern and western ends, which separate it from the east and west houses, respectively (Fig. 34). Judging from the amount of fallen stone in the other two corners of the court, there probably were no other entrances. This segregation of the south house, when the other three are continuous, might indicate that it dates from a later period than the rest of the building, and that it was built to close the open south side of the court. Such a procedure would accord well with the widespread custom observed throughout this culture area of building the community houses so that they surround interior courts.

The south house is 218 feet long east and west, and 80 feet wide. It is composed of two contiguous parts, perhaps dating from different periods, which together contain 173 rooms on the ground floor. The western and by far the larger part is made up of fourteen sections of rooms, each section running through the building from north to south. The rooms into which these sections are divided have their long axes east and west. The eastern end of the south house differs from the western end, in that its sections, of which there are four, run from east to west, and the long axes of its rooms are north and south, or at right angles to those of the larger part (Fig. 34). The manner in which this small east annex is attached to the larger western part of the building indicates that it dates from a later period of construction than the larger part. Two facts point to this conclusion: first, the western extremities of the partitions between its sections all abut against the east wall of the larger part and do not penetrate it, and, second, it extends out farther to the east than any other part of the building, and was quite superfluous so far as closing the court was concerned, since the part of the building lying west of it had already done that. Just how much time elapsed between the erection of these two parts is difficult to say, but of one thing we may feel reasonably sure, that the east annex was built later than the rest of the south house. The building material used here as elsewhere through the area covered by the Pajaritan culture is the volcanic tufa of the Jemez Plateau. This was roughly worked into building blocks usually about eighteen inches long by eight or ten inches wide and high. These tufa blocks were laid in a mortar of adobe, which was driven against them more securely by the insertion of rock spalls in the cracks of the masonry (Fig. 32). The blocks were laid in courses without reference to the breaking of joints, which, when it is found, seems to be rather more the result of accident than design. Exterior, as well as interior walls were plastered with adobe which was renewed from time to time as it wore off.

This volcanic tufa, quite aside from the fact that there was nothing else to be had, possesses three qualifications which must have recommended it to the Puyé masons as the best building material at their disposal. First, it occurs in greatest abundance in the immediate

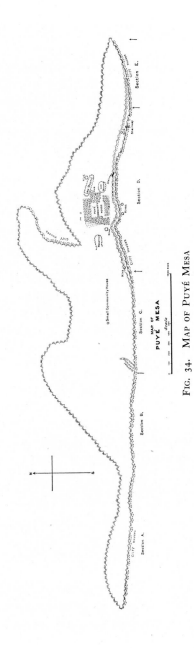

FIG. 34. MAP OF PUYÉ MESA

Fig. 35.   The South House at Puyé—After Excavation

vicinity of the building site, the whole mesa being composed of nothing else; second, it is soft enough to be readily worked with stone tools, an important consideration since the builders were unfamiliar with the use of metal; and third, it is extremely light for its bulk as well as durable. These three qualifications, of abundance, durability and ease with which their building material could be worked, are chiefly responsible for the great architectural activity of the Pajaritans, the ruins of whose villages dot the entire plateau from Shupinna to the Cañada de Cochiti and from the Jemez range to the Rio Grande.

The question as to the original height of this building, and the number of stories of which it was composed, is troublesome. At the beginning of the excavation it was clear that the fallen masonry was piled highest along an east and west line through the middle of the building from one end to the other. This would indicate that the south house was terraced from both its north and south sides, and that its several stories receded from each of these sides at the same time, until the highest was reached in an east and west line above the long axis of the building. This was corroborated during the course of the excavations, for it was found that the rooms along the court, as well as the exterior rooms along the south side of the building contained much less stone than the interior rooms, which in many cases were filled with fallen building material to a depth of five or six feet. The presence of so much fallen stone in the interior rooms and its absence in the exterior rooms indicates that above the former there had been one or more superimposed stories. This must be true since the walls of the interior rooms are now standing in most cases to their original height, about six feet, and the stone found in them must necessarily have fallen from second or third story walls above them. Other facts point to this terracing of the superimposed rooms. All fireplaces throughout the building, except in the east annex, are located in rooms not more than three or four rooms distant from either the north or south sides. Indeed, the two or three interior rooms of every section show no signs of smoke on their plastered walls, and from east to west, from one end of the south house to the other, we have a zone, the rooms of which exhibit no signs of fires ever having been built in them.

Finally during the excavation of this building fragments of the same bowl frequently were found in adjoining rooms. The only explanation of this seems to be that at the final abandonment of this pueblo such bowls were left in second or third story rooms, and when in the course of time the building began to fall to pieces, they were shattered and the fragments fell into adjoining rooms at the time of breaking. It would be hazardous to say how many stories the south house originally had. We are certainly sure from the foregoing that there had been at least one superimposed floor, and probably the amount of fallen stone found in the interior rooms would justify the assumption of another, if only composed of a single line of rooms, running east and west across the building. That there had been a fourth story, however, to this building, we may well doubt, if for no other reason than that there is hardly enough stone to have provided for the walls of three upper stories; and yet, more important, that the first floor walls now standing are not strong enough to have supported the weight of so many superimposed floors. The south house was probably an irregular pile, two, and in some places, three stories in height, which presented an appearance not unlike the modern pueblo of Taos.

It is impossible to study at first hand the method of roof construction employed by the Pajaritans in this building, as all roofs have not only collapsed, but the beams have for the most part rotted away. In the course of the excavations, however, a few roof beams were recovered, which, judging from their position and length, must have crossed the short dimensions of the rooms. Also chunks of the adobe flooring of the second and third story rooms were taken out all over the building. These were smooth on one side and on the opposite showed the impressions of the cross sticks upon which the adobe had rested.

The partitions between the sections sometimes project out beyond the north and south exterior walls of the building, making buttresses such as may be seen at some of the modern pueblos. At San Ildefonso, for example, the Indians say that these buttresses are built against the exterior walls to strengthen them. Such an explanation may well account for their occurrence at Puyé.

The rooms of the south house vary in length from twelve to sixteen feet, and in width from five to nine feet. In some cases the longer rooms have been divided in two by the erection of a partition, but in such cases the partition is probably of later construction than the building as a whole. The rooms were probably about six feet high, but as no walls now reach this height it is impossible to speak with accuracy on this point. There is a considerable difference in the floor levels in some places, those of the interior rooms sometimes being fully eighteen inches higher than the floors of the exterior rooms of the same section. Floors were made of adobe, tamped down hard and covered with a final coat of mud with which charcoal had been mixed. When this hardened it made a smooth black floor of considerable durability. The walls of the rooms were plastered with an adobe wash, which was renewed from time to time as it became smoke-blackened or scaled off. Sometimes these successive coats of adobe plaster reach an inch or more in thickness, so that when a cross-section is examined, frequently as many as ten alternating layers of brown and black appear, indicating as many renewals and subsequent blackenings of the wall finish.

Excepting doorways, the walls are pierced with but few openings. In a number of rooms, however, sometimes three feet above the floor, but more often only an inch or so from it, there are smoke holes or air vents. These are usually round, some six or eight inches in diameter. For some unknown reason the need or desire for these passed away toward the close of the period of aboriginal occupancy, and as they are now found, most of them are blocked up. The plugs used are either lumps of adobe plastered in, or shaped tufa forms like modern corks with the edges rounded off. When the tufa plugs are used they are held in place by adobe plastering. The holes which are not blocked up frequently have their sides plastered smooth with adobe and their edges rounded off. Another feature present in some of the outside rooms of this building is a ridge on the floor about two or three inches high. This crosses the short dimension of the room midway between the ends. One side of this ridge is vertical. The other reaches the floor level not by a vertical drop, but by a gentle slope, which flattens out into the floor imperceptibly. It has been conjectured by some that this latter side of the floor ridge served as a head rest, and that in it we are to see simply a primitive pillow. In accordance with this identification the name "sleeping ridges" has been applied to them.

Perhaps the most interesting feature of the south house rooms is the fireplace, the chief use of which doubtless was for cooking. There are three essential parts to the fireplace as it is found at Puyé: (1) the stone andirons or firedogs, (2) a stone against the back of the fireplace of the same height as the firedogs, and (3) a screen built upon the side of the fireplace nearest the doorway. The fireplaces are all of one type, differing only in detail, such as the number of firedogs, either two or three, and the character of the screen. In Fig. 36 there is figured the commoner type of fireplace, with two firedogs. Against the back may be seen the stone mentioned above. This latter, with the two firedogs in front, formed a three-legged support upon which the cooking stone rested. The fire was built below it, and the tortillas and other cooked dishes of the Pajaritans prepared on top of it.

The fireplaces are usually about three feet wide and half as deep. The bottoms are three or four inches below the floor level. When excavated all of them were found to be filled with fine white wood ash, which had bedded into a hard white clay. Below this level of ash the adobe of the floor is burned to a brick. In Fig. 36 the screen appears just beyond the fireplace, between it and the door. This screen, which is found with practically all fireplaces, is built so as to shield the fire from draughts coming through the doorway. It is found in two different forms. The rarer type, Fig. 36, consists of a single slab of stone, two or three inches thick, two feet high and projecting from the wall to the front edge of the fireplace, a distance of eighteen inches or more. The commoner form consists of a wall built of stone and adobe about two feet high and six inches thick, projecting from the wall to the front of the fireplace as in the other type. These screens no doubt deflected the draughts coming through the doorways and made the fireplaces draw better. One fireplace has three firedogs instead of two. This variation is rather uncommon, and was noted in but few cases. The stone at the back of the fireplace, for supporting the cooking stone, is here replaced by a flat stone which has been plastered against

Fig. 36. A Usual Type of Fireplace at Puyé, with Deflector

Fig. 37. Bins Built of Stone Slabs in a Puyé Room

FIG. 38. PUYÉ DOORWAY RAISED ABOVE FLOOR; SMOKE VENT AT LEFT

FIG. 39. DOORWAY WITH CURVED LINTEL AND SILL, IN PUYÉ DWELLING

the back with adobe. This variation of the back stone occurs about as frequently as the projecting stone, shown in Fig. 36. It allowed the cooking stone to rest upon it more firmly than did a single stone support. The location of the fireplaces in the south house is exceedingly regular. They never are found in the exterior rooms on the court or north side, and in but two of the rooms on the cliff or south side. These two latter places are somewhat irregular, in that the rooms in which they occur are only half-size, being formed by later divisions of larger rooms. Again, fireplaces are never found in the four or five interior rooms of any section. This, coupled with the fact that the two or three interior rooms of all sections never show signs of smoking on their walls, is significant as to the position of the superimposed stories. Fireplaces are not found in interior rooms because of the fact that it was above these rooms that the superimposed floors were located, and it was more or less necessary to have the rooms in which fireplaces were built communicate through holes in their roofs directly to the outside so as to provide suitable ventilation.

The two zones of rooms containing fireplaces, however, are quite clearly defined. When present they are always to be found in the second, third, or fourth rooms from the ends of a section, and in this position extend in two irregular zones, one along the north side of the building and the other along the south side.

Finally, fireplaces are always built against the walls which are nearest the outside. That is, fireplaces of the northern rooms are built against the northern walls, and fireplaces of the southern rooms against southern walls. A few of the rooms containing fireplaces have, in addition to the screen above described, an additional wall at right angles to it, and of about the same height. These two form a little vestibule, usually about three feet long by two feet wide, into which the doorway opens. Their purpose was to further obstruct air currents from interfering with the fires in the fireplaces.

Aside from these vestibules there are almost no other constructions built in the rooms. One room, however (Fig. 37), in the eastern part of the building, has three bins made of stone slabs. The doorways in the south house, as in all Pajaritan structures, are small, usually not more than two or two and a half feet high, and fourteen or sixteen inches wide. The sills are about two feet above the level of the floors, and are usually made of heavy slabs of basalt. Basalt is not found naturally on the Puyé Mesa and must have been brought from some distance at great labor, as single sills often weigh as high as fifty pounds. Sometimes, instead of these flat slabs of basalt, metates, or grinding stones, are used. A beautiful example of this latter type of sill is figured in Fig. 40, where the curve of the upper surface of the metate appears clearly. In a few places, as in the doorway in Fig. 39, for example, tufa blocks were used for sills. In such cases the block has been slightly curved, as appears in the figure. The jambs of the south house doorways are usually plastered with adobe (Fig. 38), and the edges neatly rounded. The lintels are tufa blocks, usually flat, as in Fig. 40, but sometimes concave, as in Fig. 39. In a few of the doorways the lintels were made of wooden sticks plastered over with adobe, but this type is uncommon. Many of the doorways in this building have been blocked up like the air holes mentioned elsewhere.

This tendency to do away with openings in the wall, both small and large, is marked throughout the building. For some reason there arose a desire to seal both doorways and airholes. The partial blocking up of doorways, making them smaller by raising the level of the sill, is but another expression of the same idea. The location of the doorways in the south house is important, as indicative of the probable sequence of growth in the building. Barring the doorways of the east annex to be examined in detail shortly, not a single doorway in the entire building is located in an east or west wall, or, in other words, on the ground floor there is no communication east and west between sections. Now it will be remembered that in the east annex the long axes of the rooms are changed, and that the sections in this part of the building run from east to west, so that to have no communication between sections of the east annex there must be no doorways in its north and south walls. This condition prevails except for one doorway in the south wall of Room B. This is the only example in the south house of direct communication between sections. A possible explanation for this violation of such a well grounded architectural principle is that the wall between rooms B and C, which continues out to the east end of the building, is of later erection, and that originally rooms B and C were one room, and similarly the four rooms east of them were formerly two rooms. This hypothesis is somewhat strengthened by the fact that rooms B and C, together, are about the same length as the rooms of the other two sections of the east annex. The doorway in the west wall of Room D (Fig. 40), if regarded as belonging to the room just west of D, is also an exception to the principle above stated. There is another explanation, however, for this apparent irregularity. It may be remembered that at the beginning of this article it was suggested that the east annex is of later date than the rest of the south house. If this be true, at one time the wall through which this doorway passes was the east exterior wall of the building. At that period it is highly improbable the doorway in question had been built, and the eastern wall doubtless contained no entrances. Later the east annex was built against what was then the eastern end of the building and a doorway was cut through from Room D. However, still later, the need for such a doorway passed, and when Room D was excavated its doorway was not only found to be blocked up, but was so completely plastered over that its existence was discovered only by accident.

A general view of the south house after excavation, taken from the southeast corner looking slightly north of west, is given in Fig 16. Just back of the excavated rooms of the south house the court appears as a long, dark band, beyond which the fallen masonry of the west and north houses may be seen as irregular piles of stone. The question finally arises: What were so many cell-like rooms for? Which were the sleeping rooms? Which the cooking rooms? Which the store-rooms? In short, what do we know about the house life of the Paja-ritans? Since tradition is silent concerning such intimate details of this long forgotten people, we must base our reconstruction of their life upon the results of excavation.

In the excavation of the south house it became apparent that all parts of the building did not yield specimens in equal number, that in addition to two fertile zones, there was one decidedly barren zone. This latter was composed of the three or four interior rooms of every section throughout the building from west to east. The rooms which yielded the best "finds" were, on the other hand, the three or four exterior rooms of every section along the north and south sides of the building. The best explanation of this condition seems to be that this barren zone through the middle of the building is made up of the dark rooms which were under the superimposed floors. A glance at Fig. 35 shows that the great majority of these rooms had no doorways in their walls and that consequently they must have been entered by trapdoors in their roofs. These rooms, unfitted by darkness as well as insufficient ventilation for habitation, were doubtless used as storerooms. The outer rooms north and south of them in each section are the rooms containing the fireplaces, the sleeping ridges and the doorways. These are the rooms in which the Pajaritans lived. Here they prepared their meals and here, if our identification of the sleeping ridge is correct, they slept. Trapdoors in the roofs of these rooms opened directly to the roof; ventilation was perfect, and light plentiful. In the dark interior rooms was probably stored the food harvested in the summer and fall for use in winter. Such an explanation well accounts for the scarcity of specimens in these interior rooms. On the other hand, if they were filled with ceremonial objects, as are the dark interior rooms of the modern pueblos, this is the kind of material which the people would carry away with them when they departed, again satisfactorily accounting for their barrenness.

Most of the specimens taken from the south house are such as would be used in the early life of a primitive people—grinding stones, axes, awls, bowls, water jars, and cooking pots, the kind of material that could be readily duplicated. Consequently when the abandonment came, these were left behind and the more sacred objects carried away to the new home.

•

Excavations at Puyé in subsequent years have resulted in clearing the east house, less than half as large as the south house, and in the excavation of about one-third of the west house. The north house remains untouched, reserved for study by a future generation of archaeologists. A considerable amount of work has been done on the villages at the base of the cliff. This was the first work done on ruins of this class in the Southwest. It made known a class of ruins to which I gave the name "talus pueblos." They constitute a large proportion of the ruins of Pajarito Plateau. Their study clarified some problems

FIG. 40. A TYPICAL DOORWAY, PUYÉ

FIG. 41. CLAY ARTIFACTS AND SMALL SMOOTHING STONES OF PAJARITAN TYPES

FIG. 42. GRINDING APPARATUS: METATES AND MANOS

FIG. 43. CLAY PIPES FROM PAJARITO RUINS

in Southwestern archaeology. The so-called "cavate lodges" are, for the most part, back rooms of terraced houses built on the ledges against and upon cliff walls. They are cliff dwellings as definitely as are those built in caverns of the San Juan drainage. Two of these talus villages were excavated on the slope at the base of the vertical cliff just below the great community house above described. Above this, on the second ledge of the cliff wall, two other villages of similar character were cleared.

In the course of our excavations, 4,270 museum specimens were recovered. These remains indicate that each family was provided with its own domestic equipment, such as stone mills for grinding maize; mortars and pestles for crushing seeds; implements of stone, bone, and wood; and pottery for domestic and ceremonial use.

The excavations produced some remarkable articles in stone. Among these may be mentioned the perforated discs, or stone rings, of which our excavations in 1907 produced three specimens. These rings are from fourteen to eighteen inches in diameter and about six inches in thickness (Fig. 44). In connection with these we found numerous balls of tufa from one and a half to three inches in diameter. I believe this to be identical with the equipment used in the ball game (*pelota*) of the Aztecs of ancient Mexico and the Maya of Central America. In those regions the ring was a massive disc several feet in diameter and decorated with symbolic carvings. I found these without decoration in my explorations in the Chihuahua inland basin in Mexico in 1906, and the Puyé excavations brought them to light still further north by five hundred miles. These of the north are smaller and simpler than those of the far south, but I consider them a rudimentary form of the same thing. If this is correct, we have given this ceremonial game a range of over two thousand miles. The ball courts, however, have not been located at Puyé.

In the excavation of the south house we recovered in two places, sets of ceremonial articles of stone. These consisted of idols (Fig. 45); fire stones (Fig. 31); and ceremonial knives and points of obsidian. We found, also, numerous other articles of ceremonial and domestic use. Similar specimens of these objects were found in various ruins of the plateau. A mountain lion fetish (Fig. 22) made of alabaster;

pipes (the ceremonial pipe is invariably a straight tube; Fig. 43);
flutes and whistles made of the leg bone of the wild turkey; awls made
from the bones of various mammals and birds (Fig. 28); and grooved
axes and hammers made of various minerals (Fig. 8).

The specimens recovered from Puyé are to be seen in the State
Museum at Santa Fe, where a room in the Palace of the Governors
is dedicated to the culture of this ancient community; in the Southwest Museum in Los Angeles, where the collections obtained in 1907
are deposited; and in the small field museum on the ground at the
base of the Puyé cliff where, in addition to the cultural material
derived from the excavations, a display of the plant life of the region
and of the minerals used in the manufacture of articles for domestic
and ceremonial purposes may be seen.

The northern section of the acropolis east of the great community
house yielded the skeletons of 171 individuals. These, with a smaller
number from the southern section and a few found in the caves below,
afford a basis for determining the relationship between the ancient
people of the cliffs and the modern communities of the Rio Grande
Valley. The skeletal material is all deposited in the United States
National Museum.

The pottery of Puyé will be described in a later chapter, along
with that from other ruins of the plateau. A series of sketches of the
cliff, designed to illustrate the distribution of what in all probability
were clan villages, was made by Mrs. Adelaide Chamberlain Law.
The illustrations of Puyé pictography, to be considered later (Figs.
62 and 63), are from photographs made by my former associate in
this work, Richard H. Powell.

### III. Excavations in El Rito de los Frijoles: The Old Keresan Homeland

The part of the Rito de los Frijoles of especial interest to us is
the lower five miles of its course, and of this portion a stretch covering less than two miles has the archaeological interest which claims
our attention at the present moment. The flood plain in the bottom
of the canyon nowhere exceeds an eighth of a mile in width. The
streamlet which issues from the Jemez Mountains, ten miles above,

FIG. 45. ANTHROPOMORPHIC IDOL FROM PUYÉ

FIG. 44. STONE RING USED IN ANCIENT BALL GAME, PUYÉ.

FIG. 46. MANOS AND SMOOTHING STONES OF PAJARITAN TYPES

FIG. 47. A BURIAL AT OTOWI

carries its waters during the entire year to the Rio Grande. It is never-failing. It has endured for ages through the progressive desiccation that has extended over the entire Southwest, leaving the valley of the Rito one of the few spots still habitable in a region long-since depopulated.

A glance at the outline map (Fig. 51) will give a fairly clear impression of the geological structure of the canyon of the Rito. The northern wall is a vertical escarpment three hundred to five hundred feet high, rising above a sloping talus. The southern wall has a more gentle slope and is lightly timbered.

The ancient remains in the Rito consist of four community houses in the valley and one on the mesa rim near the southern brink of the canyon, and a series of cliff houses extending for a distance of a mile and a quarter along the base of the northern wall. These cliff houses are of the excavated kind. Thirteen of the talus villages were identified and sufficient excavating done to lay bare foundation walls establishing the existence of houses of from two to four terraces built against the cliff.

Nowhere else are the talus pueblos so well preserved as in the Rito. Here we see not only the rows of holes in which rested the floor and ceiling timbers of the buildings, but in many cases the plaster is still on the rock which formed the back wall of the house in front. Of the thirteen talus pueblos, some contained not to exceed twenty to thirty rooms. The largest, shown in Figs. 51 and 52 as Group D, was a continuous house, one to four stories high, extending along the cliff for a distance of seven hundred feet. Whether each separate village represents the abode of a single clan, or whether their separation is merely dependent upon the structure of the cliff, is not known.

The Sun House was so named because of the prevalence of the sun symbol on the face of the cliff above it. This symbol consists usually of an etching of concentric circles which in most cases appear to have been painted red. The roughly crescent-shaped terrace on which the house stood is 150 feet long; its width varies from ten to fifteen feet. The western half of the terrace is only wide enough for a walk in front of the house, but the eastern half widens to a broad ledge which accommodated a small plaza.  This plaza terrace is about four feet higher than the level of the walk.  Both terraces are supported by retaining walls of unshaped tufa blocks.

Previous to excavation, no house walls were visible above the talus.  This is one of the problems in the study of the talus towns.  The condition of ruins in the valley or on the open mesas is easily explained.  Houses several stories high may crumble to the earth, and the natural drift of soil, atmospheric deposition, climatic action, and the advance of vegetation, may convert the site in the course of a few centuries to grass-grown mounds.  But with the talus houses, there is the shelter of the cliff rising in some cases to hundreds of feet above the ruins.  In some instances there have been slides of heavy rock masses from above, detached by natural weathering, or perhaps seismic disturbances, to cover the buildings.  But usually the mass which constitutes the talus ruins consists only of the debris of their own walls, covered with the detritus of natural disintegration of the cliffs and atmospheric deposits, varying with the situation of the ruin with respect to shelter.  There is, too, a considerable wash of soil from the talus, tending to keep down the amount of accumulation.  Yet buildings from one to four stories high have crumbled into the talus slopes, and have been so smoothed off that all appearance of ruined walls is wanting until laid bare by the spade.  While these are conditions which do not afford any accurate basis for estimate, they must be given some weight in any consideration of the time element in this culture.

The Sun House is the smallest of the talus villages that have been cleared.  Before excavation, eleven cave rooms were visible at varying levels above the talus.  These were, for the greater part, back chambers of the house built against the cliff.  They were nearly all on second or third floor levels.  Excavation laid bare the rooms shown on the ground plan from A to P inclusive (Fig. 52).  These are also on different levels.  Rooms A to K are in alcove form; they were mostly first and second floor back rooms made by excavating the base of the cliff, the front of the rooms and in some cases part of the sides being house walls of masonry.  These alcoves were not always on exactly the same level as the constructed rooms in front.  The rooms from L to P were built entirely in front of the face of the cliff.  It is probable

FIG. 48.  STONE KNIVES AND SMALL SMOOTHING STONES

FIG. 49.  POLISHING STONES

Fig. 50.  El Rito de los Frijoles: Indian Women Filling Their Water Jars

that these had no superimposed stories and that all the alcove rooms, A to K, had.

We thus have a total of twenty-eight rooms, exclusive of small alcoves and niches. The original number of exterior rooms cannot now be determined. Owing to irregularity of the cliff, the complete plan of construction cannot be traced. It would be safe to estimate that the Sun House, when occupied, comprised from forty to fifty rooms of all classes; that is, cave rooms, those entirely inclosed in natural rock walls; alcoves, those partly inclosed in cliff walls; and exterior rooms, or those inclosed either wholly or in part by walls of masonry. Doubtless, among the exterior rooms were some having only half-walls separating one from another, some being nothing more than open porches.

A number of rooms had the usual appurtenances of domestic life, such as fireplaces, niches, and storage alcoves. The cultural remains recovered included articles of stone, bone, wood, and clay. All rooms presented the usual appearance of dwelling chambers with the exception of B. This one, about eight by eight feet in dimension, was almost subterranean. It was sunk in the rock ledge a considerable depth below the surrounding rooms and had the appearance of having been a clan kiva. It was the one in which the lower ladder rests in Fig. 54. The upper part of the wall was probably completed by a few courses of masonry, giving the room a depth of seven to eight feet. The floor of Room K, above and back of B, was only a step above the roof of the latter. K was an alcove, three sides formed by the cliff wall, with probably an open or half-walled front. Above K was Room 2, its floor about at the roof level of K. It could have been entered from the roof, or by means of a ladder through the roof of K. A porch may have been built in front of 2, on the roof of K. Room 2 was equipped, as K and B were not, with fireplace, niches, and storage alcove. It was evidently the main living room of the group.

We had here an interesting assemblage of rooms: at the bottom, a kiva, adequate only for the use of a small clan; above this, an open room, the clearing of which yielded some objects of a ceremonial character, among them fine specimens of ringing stones which, when tapped with stones of the same kind, give out a clear metallic sound that can be heard for considerable distance. These stones, suspended from the roof by thongs of deerskin, were used to call the men to the kiva. I found this device in use in one of the kivas at Taos in 1896. Above the open room the necessary living chambers completed the dwelling.

From the landing at the base of the cliff from which the stairway turns to the right to ascend to the Sun House, another stairway turns up to the left of the western section of Group E, which, after clearing, we named the village of the Snake People. The cliff is here so irregular that no plan of the village is possible. The line where the talus meets the wall rises steeply from the common landing between the two villages, with ruins of cave houses all along, until the apex is reached about two hundred feet to the west. The chambers at the top are at least sixty feet higher than those nearest the landing. The highest rooms are those at which the upper ladder is seen in Fig. 56. From here the slope breaks away precipitously to the left for a distance of about two hundred feet, which can be passed only by means of long ladders and stone stairways. No cave rooms exist along this level, but the foot of the trail terminates at a landing eighty feet lower down, directly in front of the largest cave kiva that has been found. This is not now considered a part of the Snake Village group, and will be described separately.

The slope from Snake Village to the valley is so broken and precipitous that almost no talus exists there. Only at the point shown in Fig. 54 is there any ledge upon which rooms could be built exterior to the cliff. Here were outside rooms partly cut from the rock and in part built with artificial walls. There is space only for a rock stairway leading to the upper section shown in Fig. 56. Such is the ruggedness that only open porches could have been built in front of the cliff chambers at this level.

All the cave rooms were cleared, and ladders constructed both inside and out, so as to make them accessible. They are at different levels, and at some places two-story verandas have existed in front. All the rooms between the two ladders shown in Fig. 56 have interior connection. There are seven in the series. The passageways in front were excavated, and from the highest rooms one looks down upon a singular foreground. The slope has been sculptured by wind erosion into a grotesque group of cones and cylinders. Some of the conical masses are of great size. From the valley below, the entire village is almost hidden from view by them. Directly in front of the section where the ladders are seen is a circle of cylindrical columns inclosing one central shaft. There is some appearance of artificial shaping here, and the place strongly suggests a shrine. Such a freak of nature could not fail to impress the Indian mind with superstitious awe.

The upper section of the group is interesting mainly for its unique situation. The lower section affords much more that is instructive. The central feature is the Snake Kiva. Its position is shown in Fig. 55. This is of the class that we have named "cave kivas," it having been inclosed entirely within the walls of the cliff. A considerable part of the front had fallen away. Vestiges remained of the main entrance, which was near the center of the south side. To the right of this were traces of the ceremonial opening—which exists in all ancient kivas of the Pajarito Plateau. The shape of the room was that of an irregular oblong. Upon the floor was a row of holes—a feature to be found in nearly every kiva that has been studied in this region. These varied from three to five inches in diameter and from six inches to a foot in depth. They were placed in a straight line, about one foot apart. This distance varied slightly in the different kivas which were examined, but the number of holes was always six or seven. In this kiva there was one row only (Fig. 60). In a number of others there were two rows forming an angle, the degree of which was variable (Fig. 59). In a number of cases the holes were found partially filled with compact adobe mortar, into which were set loops of willow or other tough flexible wood, extending a little above the surface of the floor. Their function was that of loom support. A pole was lashed to the loops on the floor and another to the roof above. Then a loom was strung upon which ceremonial paraphernalia was woven. Weaving for ceremonial purposes is still done in Pueblo kivas.

Another hole, isolated from those in the rows, was found in the floor of nearly every kiva. In each of these a post was set. It always occupied a definite position with reference to the ceremonial opening in the kiva wall through which the sun's rays, entering and falling upon the post, produced a shadow which served to mark time. That it had such a function, I have been informed by trustworthy Tewa of the villages of Santa Clara and San Ildefonso.

The walls of the Snake Kiva were covered with a dense coating of smoke which partially obscured the mural decorations. A dado painted in red to a height of about forty inches extended around the interior wall. Above this was a frieze, about a foot wide, in which there was to be seen rather dimly a painting of the Plumed Serpent, the feature which gave name to the kiva. The painting is so thoroughly blackened that its original color cannot be ascertained.

Small etchings of the Plumed Serpent were found under successive washings of color upon the wall. In the small alcove to the right of the kiva, a deposit of ceremonial objects was found. Among the specimens were fragments of the framework upon which was constructed the magic snake used in connection with certain occult ceremonies, such as those observable among the Hopi. It was our surmise that here in the rooms adjacent to the kiva was the dwelling of the priest who had charge of the rites of the sanctuary.

Some distance above and to the left of the Snake Kiva, in a small alcove, was found the best specimen which was recovered, illustrating the mode of burial here practiced. On the floor of the cave, covered to a depth of two feet in volcanic ash, were the desiccated remains of an individual who had about reached the age of maturity. The body was placed on the face, with head toward the west, and was folded in the embryonic position: that is, with the knees drawn up against the chest in the position of birth. The skeleton was almost completely articulated. The body had first been wrapped in a white cotton garment, probably the dress worn during life. It was of firm texture and good weave, and large portions were in a fair state of preservation. The outer wrapping was a robe of otter or beaver fur. The robe was made by first twisting a small rope of yucca fiber about an eighth of an inch in diameter; then with the shredded fiber of eagle or turkey feathers, the fur was bound upon the cord, producing a rope of about a quarter-inch in diameter which was then woven into a robe with very open mesh. It seems probable that this was a customary mode of wrapping the dead, but the wrappings are usually decayed. Fragments were recovered in cemetery burials, but not until crypt burials in the talus villages were discovered was the material found in good state of preservation.

The situation of the large cave kiva was mentioned above. As it is not embraced within the bounds of any village, but stands completely isolated, it has been conjectured that it was for community rather than for clan use. It is almost circular in form, entirely inclosed within the walls of the cliff. Our entire force of Indian workmen, numbering as many as eighteen at a time, found in it ample room for sleeping. As it was the best example of its type that had been discovered, it was deemed wise to restore it as an example of this form of sanctuary. The floor was cleared, revealing the rows of loops described in connection with the Snake Kiva (Fig. 60), and also the remains of a firepit. The position of the altar was determinable, as was also that of the ceremonial entrance and main doorway.

The most picturesque object in the Rito is the great Ceremonial Cave. This is situated at the upper end of the formerly inhabited part of the valley, about two hundred yards above the western end of Group A. It does not mark the extreme upper limit of occupancy; straggling cave ruins are found several hundred yards farther west. On the bench across the creek, directly south, is the ruin of a small pueblo to which, following Bandelier, was given the name, House of the Water People. The cave is 150 feet above the water of the creek, made accessible by the building of ninety feet of ladders and two hundred feet of rock trail and stairway. The first ladder, twenty-five feet in length, was placed at some distance to the left of the cave. By means of this a level was reached along which, by cutting a trail in the rock, and building hand rails and stairway to a height of another twenty-five feet, the second landing was reached and upon which was placed another ladder. This was forty feet in length and led to another landing along which a trail was built to the foot of the upper ladder. This was twenty-five feet long and reached a point from which a path was constructed to the floor of the cave, thirty feet above.

The buildings which formerly occupied the cavern are destroyed, but their foundations can still be traced, as well as the imprint of their walls upon the roof of the cave. They were built of stone, some one and others two stories high, with excavated chambers at the back. The roof of the cave formed the roof of the second story, as shown in the reconstruction (Fig. 27). The plan as worked out gives a total of twenty-two rooms in the pueblo occupying the cavern. It seems likely that additional rooms occupied the eastern quarter. In the floor of the cave was found one of the best preserved and best constructed kivas of the region. This we cleared of its accumulated debris, finding numerous articles well preserved because of their protection from the elements. Specimens of matting were taken from the kiva in an almost perfect state of preservation, also perfectly preserved grains of red corn. This is one of the few ceremonial caves found in this region.

The principal focus of population was the great community house of Tyúonyi. This was a terraced structure, roughly circular in form. It was built of blocks of volcanic tufa. The amount of debris indicated that it was a three-story pueblo. Unlike the majority of large community houses of this region, this building was somewhat regular in construction. As a rule these buildings seem to have grown by gradual accretions, single rooms or suites of rooms having been added to the building to meet the needs of increasing families. Here it would appear that the entire building was planned and built at once. The curving walls were not produced by simply changing direction from room to room. The walls form curved lines. The thinnest part of the structure is at the southwest, where there is a flattening in the roughly circular plan, due to the nearness of the creek.

The building is not as well constructed as some that have been excavated in the Pajarito region, for example, those at Puyé. The walls are lighter, the stones hardly so well prepared—not so well laid nor so well plastered. The form of the building was well calculated for defense. The living rooms were entered from the inner court by means of ladders ascending to the roofs and then, through hatchways and by ladders, descending into the interior. The court, so far as can be determined, was entered by a single passageway on the east side (Figs. 19 and 20). It is of irregular width, varying from six to seven feet, the side walls covered with adobe plaster and the eastern or outer end provided with a double system of barricades. Posts were

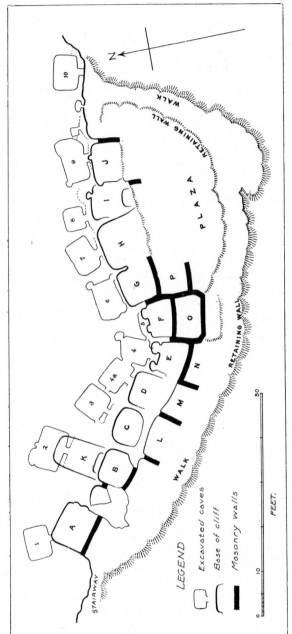

Fig. 53. Ground Plan of Sun House, El Rito de los Frijoles

Fig. 54. The Sun House—After Excavation

Fig. 55. Lower Section of Snake Village, El Rito de los Frijoles

planted across the passage at short intervals. Outside of this a stone wall partially closed, and as occasion required, could be made to completely close the entrance.

The construction of the building is such that there has been little wash of soil into the inner court, yet the exploratory trenches leading from the center toward the inner wall show an accumulation of soil in the court, since the abandonment of the building, of from two to six feet in depth—the greatest being at the southeastern part. A study of the environment of the pueblo reveals no means by which the soil could have been laid down except by atmospheric deposition. The situation is not exposed to drifting desert sands, being in a sheltered verdant canyon which lies between lightly timbered, grassy mesas.

Three kivas were found within the court, one of which we excavated. A few rods below the large community house is the largest kiva that has been discovered in the valley. It long passed for a reservoir. Excavation laid bare a circular room almost forty-two feet in diameter, lined with a double wall of tufa blocks. Near the east side was a firepit. In the floor were holes in which stood the four columns that supported the roof of the kiva. Entrance was through a trapdoor in the roof. If there was an altar it was probably between the firepit and the adjacent wall. This conjecture is based on what exists in similar sanctuaries now in use in various pueblos of the Rio Grande Valley. In three kivas excavated in the Rito, the altar—if it ever existed—had disappeared.

In the wall back of the firepit was a tunnel forming a passageway from the kiva to a shaft a short distance outside the kiva walls. The tunnel was somewhat more than two feet wide; its floor, a few inches above the floor of the kiva; and its roof, which was probably of wood, nearly four feet above the floor. On each side of the opening was a stone post, and above, a lintel of stone. The shaft was not large enough to permit of its having been a practicable entrance or exit, though the tunnel was of ample size. In the kiva here described two such openings existed, one on the eastern and one on the western side. This feature is common in ancient kivas of both the Rio Grande and San Juan valleys. It does not exist in those of the modern towns. It is what Dr. Fewkes called a ventilator. I do not accept his determination, and for the present continue to call it the place of entrance and exit for the spirit beings—which is not my conception at all, but that of half a dozen old Indian informants who knew what they were talking about.

In the Rito, kivas are found in three situations, namely, contiguous to the pueblos in the valley bottom, sunk in the talus in front of cliff villages, and excavated in the walls of the cliff. It seems likely that each group or clan possessed its own kiva. There is much to indicate that the dual system of organization existed here. It is probable that the kiva above described was the sanctuary of either the winter or the summer people.

A few hundred yards to the east of the great kiva is a circular floor made of tufa blocks laid in concentric form. Many conjectures arose with reference to the function of this platform. That it could have been a threshing floor was rejected for the reason that the natural earth, properly smoothed and beaten, forms the best possible threshing floor in the Southwest. Its function was settled for us at last by Santiago Martinez of San Ildefonso, while assisting with the excavations. Here is the field note that recorded it as told at the campfire in El Rito de los Frijoles, August 12, 1910, and which was afterward read to and confirmed by him. The revelation was made spontaneously, with little questioning. The wording is a translation of his own statements, rendered as accurately as could be from memory without making notes in his presence at the time of his recital:

It is a platform for the Night Dance. We call it the *baile de rueda*. When the sun dies, the boys dance; they dance all night while the old men smoke. When the light begins to come the women dance, all the women and girls, and they dance till the sun comes. Here is where the fire is where the old men smoke. All round the boys dance. It is always in October. It is an ancient dance and not given in San Ildefonso more than once in six or seven years. Long ago we had a platform like this in our pueblo, but if we danced this now it would be in the plaza. This must be just like ours. It was a sacred place; it was inclosed by a stockade of stone. The opening was looking down the canyon. This dance could not be given in the kiva, but must be

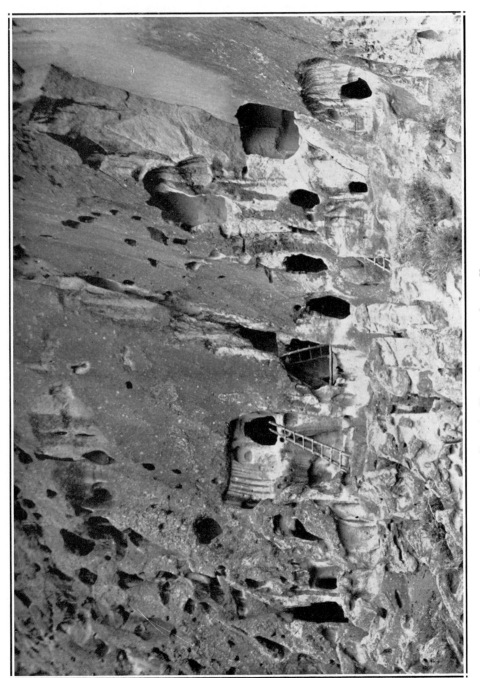

Fig. 56.  Upper Section of Snake Village

here where it would be cool. There must be a place like this, for they dance all night.

•

After some moments of reflection, he made unimportant statements not related to the dance in question. It was noticeable that he had not mentioned the men as dancing, only the boys, while the old ones smoked. I then asked why the dance was given in October, and this started a new recital as follows:

It was given when the corn was cut. There was a time when the Pueblos and the Navahos were not friends. When the corn was gathered the Navahos came to steal it. It was necessary to go out to fight Navahos. They came always by the old Wansabe trail up there. We had to kill many Navahos. When the men went out to fight Navahos, the people made the Night Dance. When the sun died the boys danced all night. The old men smoked; when the light came the women danced until the sun came, so that the men might kill many Navahos. We have this dance in our pueblo, but not often. We do not need to fight Navahos now.

•

The problem of how the people of the Rito disposed of their dead is an obscure one. It is stated by Bandelier, in *The Delight Makers,* that cremation was practiced. It is probable that this belief was based on traditions of the Cochiti Indians. Exploratory trenches carried in every direction about the great community house of Tyúonyi revealed no burial place such as we expected to find. Toward the end of our excavations, when we had almost decided to accept the cremation theory, a series of trenches through the talus in front of Group D—about two-thirds of the way down to the flood plain, carried parallel to the cliff wall—disclosed a number of burials. It seems likely that talus burial was the prevailing mode. The skeletons found were buried separately and were not accompanied with pottery or other utensils.

In one of the best preserved cliff houses of the Rito, the various articles of domestic use were restored to their proper places. In the corner adjacent to the door (Fig. 57) is seen the fireplace, with firedogs, *comal,* fire screen, and cooking pot in place as when in daily use, with the *tinaja* (water jar) and gourd dipper near at hand. In another corner (Fig. 58) are to be seen the meal box with necessary appurtenances for grinding corn, i.e., metates, manos, and *macetas.* In a small alcove adjacent to the meal box is seen the *tinajon,* or large storage vessel for the prepared meal. Above, near the ceiling and not visible in the picture, were stretched strings of rawhide on which were hung strips of drying meat, skins, and other household items. On one side of the room is the place and material for pottery making—clay, mortars, paint pots, smoothing stones, modeling forms, and vessels illustrating the various stages of the potter's art. Under the guidance of our most reliable Tewa excavators, we reconstructed a section of one of the talus pueblos. It is probably as accurate as can ever be done (Fig. 27).

FIG. 57. CORNER OF CLIFF ROOM RESTORED, TYÚONYI

FIG. 58. MEALING BINS IN CORNER OF RESTORED CLIFF ROOM, TYÚONYI

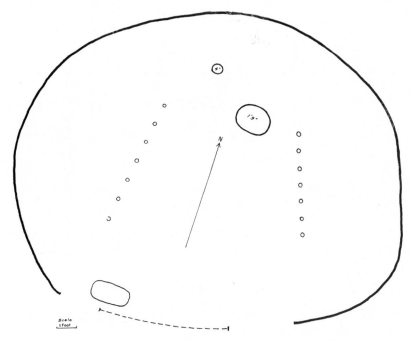

FIG. 59. GROUND PLAN, LARGE CAVE KIVA, EL RITO DE LOS FRIJOLES

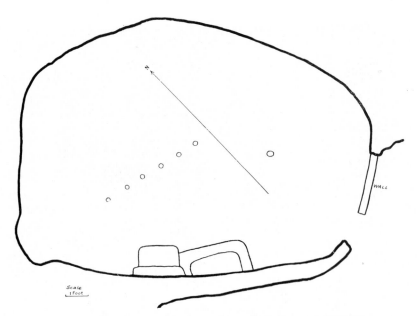

FIG. 60. GROUND PLAN OF SNAKE KIVA, EL RITO DE LOS FRIJOLES

# PART FOUR

# THE DEBRIS OF PAJARITAN CULTURE

### I. SURVIVORS OF THE ANCIENT CLANS

HE QUESTION of survival is always vital in the study of man. One would like to know to what extent the modern Greeks are descendants of templed Hellas. Are the inert fellahin of the Nile Valley scions of the mighty pyramid builders? Were the virile creators of the sacred precincts of the old Maya ancestors of the anemic dwellers of the Central American jungles of today? What relation do modern Peruvian and Bolivian Quechua and Aymara bear to the makers of the incredible ancient fortresses of the Andean highlands? Even in the absence of documentary record, there are abundant evidences to be recovered, weighed, and evaluated. That is the archaeologist's job, and the ethnologist's.

The question of survival of the humanity that once animated Pajarito Plateau has been a subject uppermost in my mind from the time of my first adventure into that silent land. It is the most pertinent problem to be faced in studying that or any other abandoned country, for survival seems to have been the first problem that man faced in his cheerless world, and the urge to survive is still the most imperative of all his problems. The sequence of my own thinking along this line with reference to the ancient Pajaritans and modern Pueblos may be here outlined.

The traditions of the Tewa of San Juan, Santa Clara, and San Ildefonso point to an occupancy of the cliff houses for a short period contemporaneous with the coming of the Spaniards. It has been found that these traditions are, in many instances, misleading.

Study of the architecture of the district discloses some interesting facts. The old caves, that is, those which are only to a small extent

99

artificial, and the small houses of stone, which are exceedingly numerous, appear to be contemporary. The newer and wholly artificial caves appear to be contemporaneous with the large terraced community dwellings, and their occupants to have been the makers of the very numerous and interesting pictographs with which the cliffs are covered. In this epoch there seems to have been a long period during which the community houses and possibly the entire district were deserted, to be occupied at a later time by people of similar culture—possibly the same tribe, but certainly of later generations. New floors were made upon a foot or more of accumulated debris, old walls were restored, old windows closed and new ones made, and a general remodeling took place. The most recent occupation of the district was certainly by the Tewa. They probably reoccupied only the artificial caves. These show some evidences of occupation by people of the same culture as the Tewa of today. The ruins of the large community houses do not show these evidences. I am inclined to think that this is the period which the Tewa point to as the time when their ancestors lived in the cliffs; that they were not the original makers of the community houses nor of the newer caves, but simply moved into ready-made homes; that their period of occupation was not of great duration, and may have extended into historic times.

In comparing a series of mortuary bowls from burial mounds at Tsirege and Sankewi'i with a number of very old pieces in the possession of Tewa Indians, mostly from Powhoge, which is but a few miles from these ruins, it was found that there were few points of resemblance. A study of over one hundred pieces disclosed little similarity. The designs of the Tewa Indians show a symbolism constant among all their villages. For example, we find the design derived from the turtle, which is so much in evidence in all Tewa mythology, to have the same significance in all Tewa towns. The same is true of their butterfly design, the design derived from the *koshare* dancers; and others peculiar to the Tewa, as well as the terraced horizon and lightning and cloud symbols common to most of the Indians of the Southwest.

Where we find evidences of recent occupation of the artificial caves, there is recognizable relationship in pottery with that of the

FIG. 61. CEREMONIAL CAVE, EL RITO DE LOS FRIJOLES

Tewa. Although in fragmentary condition for the most part, decoration conforms to that of the Tewa. This is particularly true of the latest pottery found at Puyé. The fragments with which the ground is covered in places indicate Tewa origin. Designs are to some extent biomorphic, rarely anthropomorphic.

At Tsirege and Sankewi'i there is no evidence of recent occupation except in a few artificial caves nearby. The occupants of the latter appear to have buried their dead in front of and in the caves with no accompanying pottery. In the old mounds there is noted an absence of modern Tewa designs. While biomorphic design is predominant in modern Tewa ornament, at Tsirege and Sankewi'i almost nothing of that class is found. A single zoömorph was found, and I know of but one anthropomorphic design from the entire region. Thus far the evidence points to remote relationship between modern Tewa and the earlier inhabitants.

It should not be said that the ancient people of the Pajarito were the sole ancestors of the communities now living around the margin of the plateau. That there was relationship is no longer questioned, but the degree is yet to be determined. It is the theory of absolute identity that is not accepted. This general theory concerning the ancestry of the Pueblos was first announced by Major Powell and for many years was accepted as conclusive. It was based upon similarity in culture and statements of the living Indians. My reasons for modification of this theory may be briefly stated: First, the symbols with which the ancient people of Pajarito decorated their pottery were radically different from those of the Pueblos of the present day. The symbolism of the Pajaritans was dominated by one idea. The most prevalent motive was the Awanyu or Plumed Serpent, emblem of mythic power. Awanyu was guardian of springs and streams, therefore, the preserver of life—for without water, crops, food, life must fail.

The ancient cycle of Pajaritan mythology is broken down. The merest fragments can be recovered from a few of the old men of the villages. It has been submerged by that of a recent epoch. Aside from the many variants of bird motive, the dominant religious symbol of the Pueblos of today, seen on their prayer meal bowls and etched upon the rocks, is the Plumed Serpent, still called by them Awanyu, but not identical with the Awanyu of the ancients. It is a representative figure in reptilian form with plumes upon head and body, pictured as moving through the air, and often drawn with great vigor. It is a symbol that is widely distributed over the American continent. The being which it represents was identical with the Quetzalcoatl of the ancient Mexicans. Nowhere else has it been used with such remarkable effect as upon the temple of Xochicalco near Cuernavaca, Mexico. A myth of the Tlahuicas—a branch of the Aztec stock inhabiting the Cuernavaca Valley—with reference to a mythic power represented in serpent form, and now seen in the Milky Way, is significant.

Second, convincing testimony on the subject of the relationship of the Pajaritans to the modern Pueblos is that of their physical characters. The skeletal remains which were collected, in one case as many as 125 subjects from a single burial place, have been examined by Dr. Aleš Hrdlička. In a preliminary statement he pronounced the ancient Pajaritan people to have been of rather inferior muscular development and of the dolichocephalic (long headed) type; moreover, a homogeneous people, unmixed in physical characteristics. On the same authority, modern Pueblos are a composite people with brachycephaly (broad headedness) predominating. This nonconformity of physical type interferes with the hypothesis of complete identity of the ancient cliff dwelling people with the modern Pueblos.

Evidence on which the hypothesis of identity was based was, mainly, the testimony of the Pueblo Indians themselves. The Keres of Cochiti, have always claimed the Rito de los Frijoles as one of their ancestral homes, and the Tewa of Santa Clara have, in like manner, laid claim to the ruined towns of Puyé. The claim of the latter village was taken up for thorough examination. For over a quarter of a century these Indians consistently maintained that the cliff dwellings and community houses of Puyé were the homes of their ancestors. During this period the pueblo of Santa Clara had, in the courts, a claim against the government of the United States for a large tract of land, about 90,000 acres, lying west of their grant and extending to the top of the Jemez Mountain range. The basis of the claim was an alleged Spanish grant, and in support of such documentary proof as could be adduced, their ancient homes scattered over the plateau, particularly the Puyé villages, were pointed out.

This tradition was believed in good faith by the majority of the community. It was a stock argument in pointing out the injustice of the court in granting them a strip of less than five hundred acres along Santa Clara Creek in lieu of the large tract claimed. This case was settled by setting aside the original claim and granting in lieu of it a new reservation embracing about half of the tract originally claimed. In a council held with their head men in August, 1907, to consider their opposition to my excavating at Puyé, what I believe to be the exact truth came out. They do not contend that their people, in their present organization as a village group, were the original builders of the cliff dwellings and community houses of Puyé. They hold consistently to the tradition of a reoccupation of the cliff houses and of some rooms in the great community home by the Santa Clara people during the troubled times of the Spanish occupation. It is possible that, after the Pueblo Rebellion of 1680, some Santa Clara families lived for a while in the cliff houses. This could have been but a temporary and limited occupation. The acculturation resulting from contact with European civilization could hardly have failed to manifest itself by that time in their utensils and decorative motives. The excavations at Puyé have, as yet, yielded no vestige of such influence. It is possible that the irrigating ditch along the south side of Puyé arroyo may belong to this late period.

It is true that some clans in almost every modern Pueblo village justly trace their origin to the people of the cliffs. They are a composite stock, formed probably by amalgamation of people from the cliffs with bands from outlying regions.

It is not to be supposed that the disappearance of the plateau population was due to any event of catastrophic character. Certain evidences of seismic activity have been observed, but there is nothing to indicate that the dispersion of the people was due to earthquake shocks; nothing to indicate any sudden exodus, but rather a gradual abandonment of the towns as the springs and streams dried up and the farms became untillable because of failure of the water supply. We have, as yet, no means of knowing to what distance the detachments which migrated from time to time from this plateau may have wandered. We find remnants of them at Hopi and in the villages of the Rio Grande Valley to the south, but these small bands do not account for the large numbers that must have occupied the Pajarito Plateau. Among the people nearest in physical type to those whom we have called the Pajaritans are the Tarahumara, a forest people living along the crest of the Sierra Madre and in the *barrancas* of the Pacific slope in southern Chihuahua and Sinaloa. Some California groups conform rather closely in physical type to the ancient cliff dwellers of the Pajarito. The Pawnees are of like physical type but greater stature— a difference that might have come about with a radical change of habitat and mode of life.

That I speak in this work of Puyé, Tsirege, and Otowi as ancient Tewa towns, and El Rito de los Frijoles and the adjacent region to the south as the old Keresan homeland, is evidence of where I stand on the question of former occupancy of Pajarito Plateau by ancestral clans of existing Pueblo villages in the Rio Grande Valley. It is not to be understood, however, that I accept the theory that the modern Pueblos are simply the descendants of the ancient Pajaritans. Their somatology does not support it, nor does cultural evidence. There is no continuity of symbolism. The break in form and decorative design between the ancient and modern is so radical that it can only be accounted for on the ground of strong new elements intruding from an outside source. Abrupt changes in pictography must be accounted for. Linguistic intrusions, both recent and remote, are significant, as, the linking of Tanoan with Kiowa on the east and with Zuñian on the west.

I would now go so far as to say that the ancient Pajaritans furnished strong ethnic elements that entered into the make-up of modern Tanoan and Keresan stocks—perhaps the dominant elements, especially in the Tewa. The precise mixture of breed and the sequence of modifications in culture which have occurred are technical problems for the future. The subject of Pueblo origins is a most important one, inviting intensive study in the Southwest. The resources of language, somatology, pictography, symbolism, mythology, ritual, tradition, and, to a small extent, documentary history, are yet to be integrated in this large inquiry. The student of sufficient power in gathering facts and keenness in seeing relations to make this ethnological synthesis convincingly, is being eagerly sought.

## II.  THE BOOK OF THEIR ARTS

### A. *Material Needs*

Nature was generous in meeting the needs of the ancient Pajaritans. There was stone without limit for house building, and it was right on the ground. The tufa of the cliffs, an indurated volcanic ash, was easily worked and light to handle. It was not the best of stone for masonry, but, laid in adobe mortar with ample chinking with spalls, and plastered with mud, it served well for the construction of community houses, small and large, and for the enlargement of cliff homes by the building of talus houses on the terraces and slopes. They used it successfully in construction of walls up to three and four stories which, on abandonment, soon went down to a single story of ruin buried in the debris of upper stories. The walls, unlike those of the fine sandstone in Chaco Canyon (standing after hundreds of years of abandonment to above forty feet in height), would not carry heavy roof and floor beams. Although in a country well wooded with large pine forests, only small timbers were used in construction.

Basalt from extrusions in the nearby Rio Grande Valley was ideal for metates and manos—corn grinding apparatus (Fig. 42)— and for many varieties of crushing and rubbing tools. This kind of "hardware" was recovered by the ton in all the excavations. It was not easy to carry away when the exodus came. Obsidian, many varieties of quartz, agate, jasper, chalcedony, afforded excellent flaking material for arrow points, spears, scraping and cutting blades, drills, etc. Good flint does not exist in the Pajarito region. There was plenty of the tough hard minerals that made good hatchets, hammers, clubs, and mauls. War implements were apparently not much needed. Work in stone never reached the level of a fine art as with the Mound Builders and ancient Mexicans, where form and finish were carried far beyond the requirements of utility. Even beadwork was not highly important among the Pajaritans. If they made much jewelry it did not get into the graves and ceremonial deposits.

Clays of fair quality for modeling were found in the arroyo banks—not the fine paste of ancient Hopi and Chihuahua, nor as good as that of the San Juan, but when refined of silica and volcanic sand and mixed with good tempering material (often ground up shards), it proved entirely serviceable for the making of food vessels and water jars. It was lasting, just next to stone. Large quantities of unbroken ware have been recovered from the burial places. Mineral deposits, possibly those now known near Tewa villages, and vegetable pigments, such as the black made from the Rocky Mountain bee plant (cleome), were abundant for pottery decoration. For awls, whistles, flutes, and beads there were bones of wild turkey, wild goose, and crane; while skins of elk, buffalo, bear, beaver, otter, and a few other smaller mammals furnished materials for garments, moccasins, and drum heads. Horn had its uses. Fur and feathers served in the making of burial robes. But little woodwork is found other than that used in building. In textiles, cotton produced in the Rio Grande Valley was the principal material used, but very little cloth has been recovered. Basket making was not extensively practiced among the Pajaritans at any period of their existence. Some fragments have been found in the dry caves, and a little matting with the dead. Fragments of pottery are found with basketry imprint, and a few specimens of shallow baskets have survived almost complete, fitted into the bottoms of clay vessels that have been filled with puddled ashes and used as molds in shaping new vessels. The basket debris is not confined to any one stratum. No definite stages of manufacture are apparent. In short, in the culture history of Pajarito Plateau, we have evidence of basket makers from beginning to end, but at no time of "Basket Makers"!

## B. *Spiritual Necessities (Religious and Esthetic)*

The esthetic arts of the people of the plateau were those of all ancient communities of the Southwest. Religion and art were inseparable. Almost all esthetic expression seems to have been rooted in the religious life. Their relations with the life about them called

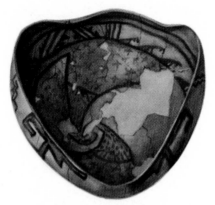

1. HEART-SHAPED FOOD BOWL
A UNIQUE FORM

2. WATER JAR WITH GLAZED
DECORATION

for some animal fetishes which were fairly well carved in the round. The Stone Lions of the Potrero de las Vacas, described in another section of this book, were their most ambitious undertaking in sculpture. One anthropomorphic idol (Fig. 45) was found at Puyé in the first year of our excavations there, and another at Otowi. The modeling of fetishes in clay was practiced in a small way, but not very skillfully.

The esthetic ambition of the Pajaritans found expression in their ceramic arts. The term "Pajaritan pottery" has been used in the nomenclature of Southwestern archaeology. If Pajarito Plateau, with its myriad rock shelters, was the original focus of ancient culture for the Rio Grande Valley—a question that can never be positively settled —then the designation, "Pajaritan pottery," will have been justified. The pottery of the Pajarito Plateau was the first of ancient Rio Grande Valley wares to become well known. In appearance it is so unlike the ancient Pueblo and cliff dwelling pottery on the other side of the Continental Divide that any novice, after a few hours of study of collections from the two areas, could distinguish between them almost infallibly. In form, color, and decorative system, the differences were unmistakable. Plate O illustrates the western slope pottery which predominates from Mesa Verde in southwestern Colorado to the headwaters of the Gila in southwestern New Mexico. Vase forms occur in great variety, and in artistic quality rival Old World ceramics. Food bowls are equally plentiful, of necessity less artistic in shape. On the whole, these artists must be accorded an eminent place in form modeling. Pottery was made by the coiling process— that is, rolling the clay between the hands into a small strand, then with this laying up the structure by continuous coiling and partially welding the overlapping coils with the fingers; then, with a scraping tool such as a hard gourd rind, shaping the vessel into the desired form.

Two decorative systems prevailed: (1) painting, with black pigment on gray- or occasionally red-slipped background, in geometric patterns, and (2) leaving the surface entirely unpainted or unslipped, incising the outer surface of the unfired vessel with a pointed implement in geometric patterns, which, in variety and beauty of design, surpass that of the painted ware. In this form of decoration the potters of this region have not been equalled. There is little in decorative motive to be interpreted, either in the painted or in the unpainted designs. It is nearly all geometric.

In describing the pottery with painted ornament, note that the term "black on gray" is used. I reject the terms "black and white" and "black on white" summarily. No one has ever seen a piece of *white* Pueblo pottery, ancient or modern. The nearest approach to it is the Mimbres ware. There is no use in perpetuating an absurdly incorrect descriptive term, even though most of the archaeologists use it. Students who are beginning to need these terms may as well adopt the correct ones. Never mind the oracles that have misguided us all these years. When it comes to choosing between a term that makes sense and one that does not, the former has it so far as I am concerned, regardless of consecrated usage.

All over this region there was an abundance of good pottery clay, with material for making paints—though of small color range—and good fuel for firing. Consequently, they were enabled to develop an art that was eminent as to both utility and beauty.

Compare now the ware above described with that on the Rio Grande side of the divide (Plates B, C, E-O). As to form in Pajarito pottery, there is little to be said, except that simple vases (water jars) and bowls (food vessels) of the most elementary character prevail, rather crudely executed by the process of coiling, entirely free-hand, no measurements, and little thought beyond utility. It was in decoration that the esthetic impulse was given rein. Ornamentation is bold and striking. The color range is much greater than in the San Juan drainage, both in paints used in producing designs and in body color of the vessels. For design painting they had black and several shades of red. The predominating ware is the black on gray. There is much black on red, especially at Puyé. There is little clear color in Rio Grande pottery, with the exception of red. The grays are dirty, never approaching white, shading into yellows that are rarely pure, as in old Hopi ware, and which run to many shades of tan and buff. In the undecorated ware there is much with corrugated surface displaying the coiling process; but there is conspicuous absence of the fine coil indented in geometric patterns which is so characteristic of the San

PLATE C

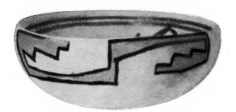

1. Food Bowl With Glazed
Decoration

2. Water Jar With Unusual
Rim Execution

Juan pottery. A micaceous wash over the surface adds a beautiful sparkle to much of the undecorated ware.

The clays were not of the best, except that used in the red ware. The gray to buff ranges from a moderately hard, fine texture to coarse, thick, and very porous ware. The latter has been named "Biscuit ware"—another "boner" in terminology.

In most of the painted decorative motives a highly developed symbolism is noted. Pictorial motives are rare. It is significant that in the older small house ruins, symbolism is almost absent. It seems to have developed with the great community houses, notably toward the close of their occupancy. After some years of effort I was able, with the help of old Tewa priests versed in their tribal lore, to get at the elements of the system of decoration that prevails. It refers mainly to a very ancient cycle of mythology, of which only fragments can be recovered. Most prevalent is the emblem of the deific power of Awanyu. This occurs in many forms. It dominates the symbolism of the entire district (see plates of Awanyu designs in accompanying envelope).

Awanyu was the principal deity in the pantheon of the ancient people of Pajarito Plateau, the antecessor of the modern Plumed Serpent to which the same name is applied. The latter is of comparatively recent appearance in the Rio Grande Valley. The former is much more archaic. The symbol begins to die out with the abandonment of the great houses. Awanyu was both a water and sky deity. Water was the essential element with the cliff people. Its abundance meant plenty, happiness, life. Its absence meant want, suffering, starvation. Hence, to keep in harmony with water and sky powers was essential. The history of the last epoch of the occupation of this plateau is one of struggle against failing nature. Existence became increasingly uncertain, life more and more precarious. It was just the condition necessary to the development of ritual and elaboration of symbolism. So we find everywhere the idea reflected in symbolic ornament upon food bowls and water jars—Awanyu, emblem of mythic power, represented by prayer plumes, by the circuit in which the power habitually moved, or by the wide band across the concavity of the vessel, the sky path of the mighty power. To the offending of Awanyu and the withdrawal of his presence was attributed the final drying up of the springs and streams and the consequent abandonment of the great houses. Awanyu, they allege, on leaving the earth, threw himself across the sky. That is what brought the Milky Way into existence. There is a variant of this myth among the Aztecs.

The striking hand-like element in Pajarito design represents the prayer plumes of the deity. It is sometimes shown as three arms whirling about a center (triskelian form), more often appended from opposite diagonal corners of the band (sky band) which extends across the interior of the bowl (Plates I and J). Occasionally, it is seen on the exterior of water jars. Symbolism relating to water is prevalent on Pajaritan water jars and food bowls. The parallel lines so often seen filling triangular spaces represent water.

There is an abundance of bird symbolism, highly conventionalized (see plates with bird symbols in accompanying envelope). Kenneth M. Chapman has given a lot of effective study to the bird motive in Pueblo design. J. Walter Fewkes made illuminating studies of it as found in Little Colorado and old Hopi ruins. Cloud and altar motives occur in the old Pajarito ware, but sparingly as compared with modern Pueblo design.

Aside from the few dominant motives above mentioned, which have been verified to reasonable certainty, we are pretty ignorant of meanings in Pueblo design, both ancient and modern. Interpretations by the young Indian potters of the present day are just about worthless—put into their heads in most cases by questioners who suggest the answers. There is an occasional pictorial design which is unmistakable, but make it a rule to go slow in *interpreting* Indian designs.

In much of the red and brown ware, as well as in the intermediate shades, found at Puyé, Otowi, and Tyúonyi, the black lines were covered with a vitreous coating which chemical analysis proves to be a true glaze. It was used solely in decoration, and while usually applied over black lines, giving the peculiar under-glaze effect, the material was, perhaps intentionally, caused to spread over large areas, producing striking effects, especially when by reason of mineral elements in the clay, rich, iridescent hues occurred. Only one specimen was found, a small prayer meal bowl at Puyé, in which the entire interior surface of the vessel is covered with glaze (Plate E, first figure). It is, therefore, not accurate to use the term "glazed ware" or "glazed pottery" in Pueblo ceramics. There is no glazed ware—only glazed ornament.

For expert advice on the subject of Pajaritan glaze, on recommendation of Dr. William H. Holmes, I put in the hands of Dr. Wirt Tassin, chemist of the United States National Museum, an assortment of shards from the Puyé and Otowi collections. These were subjected to thorough study in his laboratory and his findings were discussed with me from time to time. The following paragraph concerning the chemistry of the glaze is made on his authority and received his approval:

The process of decorative glazing, as practiced by the Pajaritans, could have been very simple. After a vessel had been decorated and fired in the usual manner, a saturated solution of salt water laid on over the painted ornament and the vessel again fired under as great a degree of heat as they were able to produce in their primitive kiln, would have caused a fusion of the sodium of the solution with the silica of the clay, producing over the design and over all surfaces on which the solution spread, a transparent glaze which could never scale or peel off without taking with it the clay of the vessel itself to the depth to which the salt water had penetrated. The spreading of the solution and the occurrence of oxides in the clay could have produced beautiful accidental effects, particularly the rich iridescent tints found on the pottery at Puyé and Tyúonyi.

It should be noticed that Dr. Tassin did not dogmatically assert that the Pajaritan glaze was so produced, but simply that it could have been. In this he has the support of eminent authority. I am aware that there has been much subsequent study of the subject with various conclusions. The terms "glaze-paint" and "glazed-paint" now much in use are far from satisfactory. Much of the so-called "glaze-paint" is just plain paint with a lustrous quality, entirely devoid of the true glazing material.

Decorative glazing was practiced in the valley of the Little Colorado. The art may have been carried there from the Rio Grande drainage or vice versa, or it could have developed independently in the two regions. Arguments as to its place of origin are, up to the present time, unconvincing. Little Colorado glaze was generally of poor quality as compared with the Pajaritan. Nowhere else on the American continent was it so well handled as in the Pajaritan region. It was long held, and may still be by some, that the art was not indigenous to America and that wherever found it is an indication of European influence. By some it has been called Spanish glaze. We have shown the contrary to be true. It was well on the way toward becoming a lost art at the time of the advent of the Spaniards and was never revived by them. It was practiced on the plateau west of the Rio Grande centuries before the discovery of America by Europeans, and ceased to be practiced among the modern Pueblos during the upheavals of the seventeenth and eighteenth centuries. The art is now unknown to the Indians of the Rio Grande Valley. It is never seen in the specimens that have been handed down among them for many generations, and it is not found in the recent refuse deposits of their villages. On the other hand, it occurs in the ruins on the Pajarito Plateau, where no vestige of European influence has been found—sites which, if occupied at the time of the conquest, could not have escaped mention in the records. It may be safely affirmed that decorative glazing was an indigenous American art.

The Rio Grande wares stay pretty consistently on their own side of the Continental Divide. True western slope wares, especially of the San Juan Valley, rarely spill over into the Rio Grande drainage, except in the minds of archaeologists bent on finding "influence" of one culture on another, or establishing "migrations" that never occurred. The archaeologist is the original "blind man in a dark room looking for a black cat that isn't there"—and finding the cat. I obtained at Cochiti, some years ago, fine examples of *San Ildefonso* pottery. There were quantities of it there. I also found the potter who made it—a San Ildefonso woman married to a Cochiti man, and living the last part of her life in that Keres town. If María Martinez, the famous potter of San Ildefonso, for any of the reasons that cause ladies to change residence—matrimony, kidnapping, elopement, and so on—should be transplanted to Zuñi, it is safe to say that there would be a revolution in the ceramic art of that community, and that the archaeologists of the future would find, in that place, evidences of a large "migration" from the Rio Grande Valley, or at least much "trade" across those two hundred semi-arid miles.

The following may be put down as a purely non-technical description of the ancient Pajaritan pottery, leaving detailed classifications to experts in that line.

1. Undecorated ware.
    a. Unpolished black ware without corrugated surface; considerable mica in the clay; much used for cooking vessels; extremely poor quality.
    b. Unpolished black ware with corrugated surface not in geometric patterns; used mainly in cooking vessels.
    c. Polished lustrous black ware; used as food bowls and water jars.
    d. Polished lustrous red ware; used as food bowls and water jars; rare.

2. Decorated ware.
    a. Gray ware tending to yellowish; smoothed; decorated with black lines in patterns usually, but not always, symbolic; occurs both in vase and bowl forms, though much more frequently in the latter. This ware, with that next mentioned, constitutes the great bulk of Pajaritan pottery that is preserved to us.
    b. Red to brown ware with glazed ornament. This is the most beautiful of all Rio Grande pottery (my opinion only; some dissent). Several shades of red were used, two being sometimes applied to the same vessel. The texture is also superior. This ware usually occurs in bowl forms, but we find it also in water jars. The glazing was handled, in many cases, so as to produce highly artistic effects. While used more at Puyé than at other Pajaritan sites, we have found specimens of it at all the sites excavated except in the small house ruins.
    c. Non-lustrous black ware decorated by incision in geometric patterns; used mainly on water jars. Some pottery lovers think this the finest of all.

It should be remembered that in this dissertation on pottery I have attempted to put down a description which the general reader can use in looking at the specimens in museum cases. I have tried to avoid technical terms and have kept away from the interminable classification of the specialists. I prefer to recognize only a few types based on obvious characteristics. It might not do the specialist any harm to practice a bit on condensation of types rather than further multiplication. The number of "types" in Southwestern pottery is becoming terrifying. They run into the hundreds. There is a "type" for about every locality and shade of color. Soon we may have one for every ruin—only a few thousand of them, and why not eventually as many types as there were individual potters? Typology is something that I cannot get excited over.

For those who would like to go into the study of Pajaritan pottery a bit more thoroughly, I recommend the memoir, "Pottery of the Pajarito Plateau and of Some Adjacent Regions in New Mexico," by Dr. A. V. Kidder, published by the American Anthropological Association in 1915. It is based largely on the collections derived by the excavations described in this handbook. It is a first-rate treatise, equally useful to the general reader and to the student of archaeology.

We are including at the end of this publication an envelope of plates illustrating Pajaritan pottery. The packet covers the collections of a number of expeditions: namely, those of the New Mexico Normal University from 1898 to 1903; my excavations under the auspices of the Smithsonian Institution in 1905; excavations by the School of American Research from 1907 to 1927; collections made under our sponsorship by Dr. L. L. W. Wilson for the Philadelphia Commercial Museum; and by coöperative excavations between the School of American Research, Bureau of American Ethnology, and the Southwest Museum.

## C.  *The Rock Picture Book*

The petroglyphs (rock carvings) of Pajarito Plateau were first studied from 1899 to 1901, while I was connected with the New Mexico Normal University. A member of the faculty, Professor R. H. Powell, now dean of the Coördinate College, University of

Georgia, photographed the examples here shown, mainly from the Puyé cliffs. These preserve one phase of the graphic arts of the Ancient Pajaritans and afford a rich field for the study of an early form of picture writing. They were etched with stone tools upon the soft tufa of the vertical cliffs. No analysis of them will be undertaken here, either as graphic art or documentary records. Students will be interested in comparing them with rock pictures in other parts of the world. They should be studied in connection with the abundant material which is being prepared for publication in another handbook of this series, *Archaeological History of the Rio Grande Valley,* especially that from Embudo Canyon north of San Juan pueblo; from La Ciénaga, about twelve miles southwest of Santa Fe, near where the Rio Santa Fe enters its gorge at La Boca; and at Comanche Gap, thirty miles south of Santa Fe on the line of the New Mexico Central railway. Unlike those of the Puyé cliffs which were cut in very soft material, and, in consequence, are much dimmed by weathering, the pictures of the other groups named were etched upon hard basaltic boulders, as durable as time, and are, therefore, but little changed with age.

There is wide scope in design in the rock art at Puyé. There are many anthropomorphic, many zoömorphic, some symbolic, and some purely geometric designs. Much of the drawing is crude, some is exceptionally well done. The naïve mode of presenting the human figure and animal pictures is particularly noticeable. Symbolism is far inferior to that of the pottery designs at Puyé. Casual comparison of this art with that of the recently discovered kiva frescoes at Kuaua, on the west bank of the Rio Grande near Bernalillo, does not give the impression that the Puyé rock pictures were intended to be ceremonial or mythological records, as are the Kuaua murals. They are a much less serious form of art, merely suggestive of the play of fancy that characterized the Indian mind throughout the Southwest, which reflected, to some extent, their attitude toward nature and life, but which had little function in recording facts. In other words, we may see here elementary steps in the evolution of art that attained to much higher levels of expression in the cultures farther south: Aztec, Maya, etc., but which, even there, remained sterile as historic records.

FIG. 62. PETROGLYPHS AT PUYÉ

FIG. 63. PETROGLYPHS AT PUYÉ

The position of the majority of the pictures on the Pajaritan cliffs, usually where they could have been made conveniently from the roofs of the dwellings terraced against the cliff walls, suggests that they belong to the period of the great community houses and of the contemporaneous talus villages. Some, however, as with the sun symbols in the Rito de los Frijoles, are in places that would have tested the daring of the artists to the utmost.

Another class of rock picture carving is found inside the cave dwellings. A study of the cave pictographs of El Rito de los Frijoles by Mr. Chapman, was reported in a paper read at the annual meeting of the Archaeological Institute of America, at St. Louis, December 29, 1916, and published as *Paper No. 37* of the School of American Archaeology. Mr. Chapman has incorporated the substance of that report in the paper herewith presented, with illustrations, as Appendix I.

### III. The Imperishable Record

Throughout the early years of my work among the Pajaritan ruins, there was no thought more intriguing than that of the religious ceremonies which I felt sure must have enriched the lives of those ancient people. With relative certainty one could re-create the domestic scenes of a thousand years ago. Life flowed as rhythmically, almost as quietly, as the waters of the mountain streams. The stage was still there and many of the properties still in place, the shadowy actors moving silently through their parts. (They were never very noisy in their virile prime.) Men went quietly to the fields or the hills to the tasks that nature prescribed according to the seasons. Maidens carried water jars on their heads from the streams to the houses of the cliffs, with faultless grace transmitted to them by generations of mothers who walked with flawless dignity. Children played on the cliff walls as nimbly and safely as the squirrels. Families squatted on their floors for the simple meal, every item known and acknowledged to be the gifts of beneficent powers. Youth found the age-long way of life. Old age blessed the people with wisdom and knowledge. Anyone fit to write human history could visualize all this awake and dream about it asleep. But those plazas of the great community houses had

once been vibrant with the rhythms of dancers and the chants of wor-
shippers—community spirits keeping time with the seasons, pulsating
through the centuries in invocation to the givers of life. One could be
sure of this, knowing something of the soul of the Indian.

To feel that all this had perished utterly was well-nigh unthink-
able. Here were the habitations, utensils, works of art—wreckage
it is true, but susceptible to restoration and almost perfect interpretation. One is reluctant to think of material being more enduring than
spirit. But here the most potent manifestations of life seemed to have
vanished. To the archaeologist of somewhat philosophic turn of mind
and deeply reverential spirit (without which qualities, one should
certainly go into some other business), this means depression, a sense
of frustration, a *qui bono* state of mind.

The way out is in getting back to the living. Witnessing the
seasonal ceremonies of the Pueblos in the Rio Grande Valley, learning
how absolutely vital they are in the lives of the people, one naturally
begins to seek for their genesis as well as their symbolic meaning.
Only one answer is ever obtainable if you question the old men to
whom these ceremonies still hold the deepest meanings of life. "Where
did we get these dances? From our ancients, amigo." "How long
have we had this dance? Always, señor." I have never known a
serious old Pueblo Indian who did not *know* that their old dramatic
festivals (I am not here considering war dances, etc., picked up from
visiting tribes) came down to them from their ancients of the cliffs.

So potsherds, or even stone hammers and flint chips, do not
constitute the most enduring record in the story of man. They are,
at best, the flotsam and jetsam of human history. The archaeologist
who believes, above all things, in the life of the spirit may take heart.
In a Green Corn Dance at Santo Domingo, a Buffalo Dance at San
Ildefonso or Tesuque, a Basket Dance at San Juan, he is witnessing
exactly what he might have seen, were he a Methuselah, centuries
ago in the plazas of Puyé, Tsirege, or Tyúonyi. Drama, I have said
many times, is the most fundamental of human arts. It is the imperishable record of the life of man.

Some years ago Marsden Hartley, artist, poet, philosopher,
came to Santa Fe and spent some months in the atmosphere of the

ancient city.  So impressed was I with his understanding of the Indian ceremonies which he witnessed that I begged him to put in writing his interpretation.  This he did in a series of short articles on the subject of "Red Man Ceremonials," which were published in *Art and Archaeology* and in my *Ancient Life in the American Southwest,* and which I wish might be studied by every reader of this handbook.

The surviving villages that partially surround the Jemez Plateau —San Juan, Santa Clara, San Ildefonso, Cochiti, Zia, and Jemez— are all on the margin of the area which was overspread by the Pajaritan culture. As explained in a previous section, this ancient culture was, to some extent at least, absorbed into surrounding communities.  This comes out most noticeably in the dramatic ceremonies.  However, as fully confirmed by the most responsible informants, there is not a village among those named that does not retain in its esoteric life today beliefs and customs which reach beyond the realm of religious ceremonies that we are permitted to witness.  It is no exaggeration to say that the Pueblo Indians live in a mystical world all but unknown, largely unknowable outside of their own clans.  While it is mainly an immaterial world, it is made tangible among themselves through myth, legend, and symbol.  These forms are elements in what I have called the Imperishable Record. The extreme reticence of these people would keep all knowledge of these phases of their culture securely held in their own minds were it not for their fondness for story telling or graphic expression through drawing and color, and for their willingness to communicate linguistic and geographical information. Investigators may well take note of this observation.  Through these channels of self-revelation, though largely by indirection, lie the avenues of approach to real knowledge of the immaterial world of the Indians.  Nothing will better illustrate this than a study of the ancient shrines and other sacred places of the plateau, within the horizon that bounds the Pueblo world.  These became known to me first through campfire tales, afterward verified by pilgrimages to the places described, further illuminated by drawings and paintings, and brought down to tangible record through conversations about geographic sites and the meaning of archaic words.

The Stone Lions of Potrero de las Vacas and Potrero de los Idolos have been previously described (page 55).

The shrines of the four world quarters are less well known. Ancient Tewa-land embraced roughly one hundred and fifty miles of the Rio Grande Valley, from San Antonio Mountain, on the Colorado-New Mexico line, on the north, to Sandia Mountain, northeast of Albuquerque, on the south, and lying between the Sangre de Cristo range on the east and Jemez range on the west. It has for its conspicuous boundary markers the four world mountains. On the east is Lake Peak *(Agatsanu piñ*—meaning obscure); on the west, Pelado *(Tsi kumu piñ*—Covered Obsidian Mountain, or Black Stone Mountain); on the north, San Antonio *(Ke piñ*—Bear Mountain); and on the south, Sandia *(Oku piñ*—Turtle Mountain).

The first named, consecrated to fertility, has, or had many years ago, its stone shrine on the top and its sacred lake where mating ceremonies of the most secret and sacred sort were still held. There has been some hazy knowledge of this, which should remain hazy, among the white people. It has been the source of much unjust, though well meant, criticism. For a couple to present themselves for marriage with a child some weeks old in the mother's arms, seems irregular to say the least. I want to say here with as much emphasis as I can that these matings, consecrated on the mountain sacred to the bringing of new life into the world, are just as legitimate as those solemnized by priest or justice and, with or without confirmation by church or civil ceremony, are to be respected as having the highest religious sanction. It is strictly in conformity to their moral law. Our Christian code with reference to marriage, or the Jewish, Mohammedan, Buddhist, or Confucian, is no more deeply rooted in the spiritual nature than is this procedure of the Tewa Indians.

The North World Mountain, Kepiñ, is, as its name, Bear Mountain, implies, consecrated to the hunt. The stone shrine on its summit has long-since disappeared. Vestiges of it were to be traced when I first saw it in 1898, and to this day, prayer meal and other sacred offerings are found on and about the site, for it is still occasionally visited by the Indians in preparation for ceremonies of the hunting season. It is not, however, as important a shrine as the Stone Lions of Cochiti, most potent of all hunting fetishes. It is gradually falling into disuse, although the mountain itself will doubtless be looked upon for all time as one of the sacred landmarks.

Pelado, the West World Mountain, is consecrated to the spirit life. Those who "go west" to the land of Sipophe, must travel over the dangerous trail that passes it on the south—a trail beset by malevolent beings. On the top is the stone shrine, or what was left of it by the zealous government employee who presumably thought it would serve some good purpose in Washington. That stolen Indian shrines, however potent they may be, will appreciably ameliorate the intellectual and spiritual condition of Washington may be doubted. The Indians miss their ancient shrine sadly. Nevertheless, the sanctity of the place remains unimpaired, and as the ghostly procession moves eternally to the land of Sipophe there is no diminution in the use of this deeply venerated shrine. It is comparable to the one on the East World Mountain, whence the new life emerges into the *Tewabuge*, while here on the west the old life serenely passes out into the shadows.

The South World Mountain, Okupiñ, with its ancient shrine, consecrated to war, has ceased to have its old-time significance with most of the Indians. Perhaps in present world conditions it might not be a bad idea if it began to function again. It is the Mount Olympus of the Rio Grande Pueblos. In the red cloud above it, always visible to every good Indian, dwells *Ok'uwapiñ,* father of deities. Here the Twin War Gods were born, and, for a long time, went about performing miracles and doing all sorts of good turns to humanity. They were twins, although one was quite a bit younger than the other. That discrepancy does not worry the Indian at all. Their attributes, supremely godlike, were yet so human that we almost see in them an analogue of the remarkable God-man that came out of Nazareth. True, these were war gods and the Man of Galilee was the Prince of Peace. Still we hear Him saying, "I came not to bring peace but a sword." Again in the temple He showed that He could handle a scourge effectively. The twins brought peace to the valley by driving out evil beings. Their weapons were not so formidable, only flint knives and bow and arrow; and in all the yarns about them we do not find them engaged in any real wars. Not world-wide did their presence extend, as did that of the Galilean, but we hear of them from Alaska to Patagonia. Not to carry the analogy further, it is interesting to note here in the New World, as well as in the Old, the Divine could be made human and the human made Divine.

*Wankwijo* (Wind Woman) also has her seat on Sandia Mountain, though so far as I know there is no separate shrine for her. She is responsible for the rather prevalent dust storms of the middle Rio Grande Valley. Perhaps she has moved of late years to western Oklahoma and the Texas panhandle and is now the presiding deity of our Southwestern dustbowl.

Spider Woman lives on Sandia Mountain. She is a beneficent deity. She it was who helped the Keres Indian to find his wife and bring her back from "Sky Pueblo" (not Acoma nor the ruined Sky Village northwest of Albuquerque, but a pueblo conceived to be up in the sky). This Indian Helen of Troy, like her Grecian prototype, early acquired the habit of being abducted. Spider Woman, when her good offices were solicited, spun a web from Sandia Mountain to Sky Pueblo, over which she and the deserted husband crossed, captured the erring lady, and brought her back home over the spider web bridge to Sandia pueblo—all without any such rumpus as was caused by the Trojan episode.

Shrines on other "high places" protect the Indian world. As with the Hebrews of old, high places were set apart for ritualistic practices by the ancient Pueblos and continue in such service to this day. I have previously mentioned the shrines on the hilltop just east of San Ildefonso, where the cacique still performs the early morning ritual. It is a large boulder with cup-like depression in which ceremonial material —shells, feathers, blue corn, and various ingredients—are ground. A shrine of this kind is to be found near almost every important ruin of Pajarito Plateau, disused since the abandonment of the cliffs. It appears to have been an essential thing in every community. A hill a few rods southeast of San Ildefonso, unmarked by any material sign, is the *Weyima oku. Weyima* is the abode of the ancient spirit people of the underworld. Seated on this little hill you can, if you are a good Indian, hear the chanting and feasting going on in Weyima.

On the top of Black Mesa (Tuñjopiñ) north of San Ildefonso and south of Santa Clara, were formerly two shrines—one, a boulder shrine still there, the other, a fire shrine constructed of lava stones, now demolished, but the site still marked by the pile of fallen basalt. "Tuñjo" is the scene of much mythology and legendry, as well as of historical incidents. Under it lived the giant, *Tsavijo*, and his family —wife and daughter. Near here he was slain by the Hero Twins and his remains lie buried under Black Mesa. Another version has it that he was trussed up by the Twins in unbreakable bonds and still lives there. His groans may be heard at times, especially when something is needed to awe bad children. The cave on the north side of Black Mesa, avoided by the superstitious Indians, was the entrance to the abode of Tsavijo. Black Mesa has figured in both prehistoric and historic sieges. In accounts of one of the latter appears Juan Archeveque, one of the murderers of LaSalle near the mouth of the Trinity River in Texas, who, with his fellow assassins, drifted west to the Rio Grande and up to Santa Fe and Santa Clara, where he was married, and finally out onto the great plains, where he died with his boots on.

The shrines of the sacred lakes are the most venerated of all. The Tewa have no doubt that the World Mountain shrines were possessions of the ancient Pajaritans. They ascribe to them, likewise, the shrines of the Sacred Lakes, pools which are still potent in their ceremonies. The pool in the sand dunes east of Alamosa, Colorado, by way of which the ancestors emerged from the underworld, has been described in a previous section (page 33). Of constant use in affording "medicine water" *(wopo)* for the rain ceremonies, are the pools of the four directions. The Sacred Pool of the East *(T'ampije pokwing)* is in a swampy place in the valley east of San Ildefonso pueblo. That of the North *(Pimpije pokwing)* is on the east side of the Rio Grande, north of the confluence of Santa Cruz Creek with the great river. Here is where the *kosa* (Keres, *koshare*) get the clay with which they paint their bodies for ceremonies in which they participate. The Lake of the South *(Akompije pokwing)* is just back of the water tank of the D. & R. G. railway ("place where the train drinks"), south of the Otowi bridge across the Rio Grande. The Sacred Pool of the West *(Tsampije pokwing)* is in a romantic spot which I hope will never become too well known, in the hills west of the Rio Grande, on the very rim of Pajarito Plateau. It would be safe to say that for a thousand years it has supplied "medicine water" for the rituals of Rio Grande Indians. The holy water of the Christian font is not one whit more sacred than is this of the Sacred Spring of the West. The pool has a function similar to that of Toreva Spring at Hopi Mishongnovi (Middle Mesa) in the Flute Ceremony. But the ritual water from the Below is brought up in small water vials of clay *(woposa)*, instead of in little gourds, as at Toreva. The priest, when he rises from the water, also brings up Awanyu with him (Plate F). The ancient pear trees over the spring, probably as old as the famous apple trees of Manzano, still live and bear fruit. Here you can see, if you are a perfectly initiated Indian, the little fairy-like creatures, Blue Man, Green Man, Speckled Man, hopping in and out of the pool and among the branches of the old pear trees. Once in a blue moon you can see the kosa sprites peeping up over the rim of the sun (see frontispiece).

The old hut of the rain priest, on the hill overlooking the shrine, has fallen down and is no longer used. Here, through many an evening, I sat at the feet of my most revered teacher of anthropology, old Weyima, rain priest of San Ildefonso, and caught some glimpses into the mystic world of the Pajaritans. It is significant that the stories, as told by him and later by his successor, Potsonutsi (Diegito), never varied from one another by so much as a word.

That springs should be among the most venerated of shrines, and the water of sacred pools be looked upon as veritable "holy water," is understood when it is known that, to the Indians of the Southwest, water is a symbol of life itself, an emanation from the Sky Father, *Makowa sendo;* the element to which Earth Woman, *Nankwijo,* owes all fertility and fruitfulness—all of which the ancients correctly worked out without any university courses in meteorology.

The above are samples of what I had in mind when I said that through the fondness of the Pueblos for story telling and facts of geography, together with the absence of tabu in discussing words and their meaning, we are able to penetrate to some extent into their esoteric world. There may be added here a few examples of what they reveal through their graphic art, largely symbolic:

1. Altar Painting: The painting herein shown (Fig. 17) is not from Pajarito Plateau nor from any Tewa town. Its symbolism, however, is as well understood by the Tewa as it is by the Jemez people, in whose pueblo the best example of this design of the *Opa* (universe) is found. It is said to be very ancient and of common knowledge among all the Pueblo villages. Herein is disclosed the essential structure of an esoteric world.

2. Paintings of Ceremonies: These paintings by young Pueblo artists, with interpretations that have come out spontaneously in conversations with the artists and older people interested in their work, have been an almost inexhaustible source of information. This is a phase of Pueblo culture that came near becoming a lost art. It was revived a few years ago, as described in one of my annual reports (1920):

In 1918, Crescencio Martinez, a Tewa Indian from the pueblo of San Ildefonso, brought to our attention a number of water color paintings executed by him, illustrating the costumed figures in certain ceremonies performed by his people. Struck by the artistic merit of these as well as by their ethnological value, we engaged him to produce, in water color, pictures of all the characters that appear in the summer and winter ceremonies. These he finished just before his untimely death. Other young Indians of his town, as well as from adjacent villages, noting that the work of Crescencio met with appreciation and remuneration, made it known that they could do similar work. This they were urged to do by the staff of the School and by the officials of the United States Indian School in Santa Fe. The result has been that a number of young people from fourteen to twenty years of age, working at the Indian School, the Museum studios, and at their own homes, have been producing paintings that command the respectful interest of the artists of this country. Their paintings are in demand for display in the best galleries of the United States, and even in European galleries.

The remarkable thing about this is not the discovery that there are artists of high ability among the Indians, but the fact that, with

FIG. 64. SNOW BIRD DANCE

*(By Velino Shije)*

FIG. 65. SAN ILDEFONSO'S SACRED POOL OF THE WEST

FIG. 66. THE SUN DANCE AS DANCED TODAY

FIG. 67. SUN DANCERS, AS PAINTED BY FRED KABOTIE

no instruction in drawing or color, they are able to produce work of such artistic merit. Their work is as definitely racial as anything that has come out of oriental countries, and although in the midst of American artists whose work they see constantly in the Museum galleries, they remain practically uninfluenced. It is not yet possible to foresee the importance of this new development in Indian art. It can be said, however, that a talent is manifesting itself in a surprising way which, with the encouragement it is receiving, may be destined to affect materially the place of Indian culture in the estimation of thinking people.

•

A number of ancient ceremonies that had fallen into disuse have been revived through interest in these paintings. One or two examples of these may be presented here:

The Sun Dance: This ceremony, formerly engaged in by practically the entire village, has come to be a dance in which the whole population is represented by two men and two women representing the two halves of the village. It is a spring dance celebrating the return of the growing season with a dramatization of the planting, cultivating, and growth of the corn as a result of the return of the sun. This ceremony had entirely disappeared from the pueblos, and was recently revived by the Indians of Santa Clara. It is almost identical with the ceremony known as the Acequia Dance, in which the principal episode of the celebration is the turning on of the water in the ditches with the advent of the planting season. The Acequia Dances of Isleta have become well known.

The Bow and Arrow Dance: This is one of the favorite hunting dances of the Pueblos, and survives in nearly all of the villages. It is a ceremony in which the whole population participated, at least symbolically, and is a dramatization of the sympathetic relationship which man has always tried to sustain with the animals of the forest. The ceremony is rich in mimicry and symbolism. The movements of hunters and of the animals hunted are all represented. Some of the formations are extremely beautiful, particularly those in which the dancers arrange themselves in the form of the great bow and arrow. Various forms of this ceremony are to be seen. In some cases it is known as the Arrow Dance. In others, some of the elements of the ceremony are merged into those that appear under other names, such as the Antelope Dance, the Buffalo Dance, the Antlers Dance, etc.

Thus in the rituals, dramas, arts of the living, the ancient Pajaritans have their "Imperishable Record," and from their abode in Weyima they come to mingle with and guide the people in the "good way." And to these Old Ones the living through unending time pay reverential homage by seeking the ancient wisdom and conforming life to the "good way" of their divine ancestors. This is the purest form of ancestor veneration—erratically called in the histories of religions, ancestor *worship*. Just another "boner" in nomenclature. Worship is homage paid to deity. These ancestral spirits among the Pueblos are *not* deities.

### IV. Minor Excavations: Otowi, Sankewi'i, and Tsirege

About five miles west of where the Rio Grande enters White Rock Canyon is the prehistoric settlement of Potsuwi'i or Otowi. To reach it one ascends the mesa by following up Alamo Canyon from its confluence with the Gaujes. The summit of the first mesa is reached at the head of that part of Alamo Canyon known as the Black Gorge. The first canyon entering the Alamo from the north above this point is the Otowi. Following this for about two miles, a point is reached where the long, narrow potrero bounding the canyon on the north is entirely cut out for a distance of nearly a mile, thus throwing into one squarish open park the width of two small canyons and the formerly intervening mesa. From the midst of this park, roughly a mile square, a view of surpassing beauty is to be had. Half a mile to the south, the huge Rincon del Pueblo bounds the valley with a high unbroken line, perhaps five hundred feet above the dry arroyo at the bottom. An equal distance to the north is the more abrupt Otowi Mesa, and east and west to about an equal height rise the wedge-like terminal buttes which define this great gap in the middle mesa. Toward each of the four corners one looks into a thickly wooded gorge. The whole area is well forested.

The parallel canyons running through this glade are prevented from forming a confluence by a ridge, remnant of the intervening

PLATE D

THE RAIN PRIEST COMING FROM THE SACRED LAKE (By an Indian Artist)

mesa. Upon the highest point of this ridge is a large pueblo ruin which formed the nucleus of the Otowi settlement. In every direction are clusters of excavated cliff dwellings of contemporaneous occupation, and on a parallel ridge to the south are the ruins of one pueblo of considerable size and six small ones, all antedating the main Otowi settlement.

The traditions of Otowi are well preserved. It was the oldest village of the Powhoge people of which they have definite traditions. They hold that prior to the building of this village they occupied many of the scattered small houses of the adjacent mesas. They know that when the mesa life became untenable from lack of water, and removal to the valley a necessity, a large detachment from Otowi founded the pueblo of Perage in the valley on the west side of the Rio Grande, about a mile from their present village. Their ancient sacred spring, Tsampije pokwing (sacred pool of the west), lies in the hills less than a mile southwest of Perage. It is the best preserved of their four cardinal rain shrines, still used in connection with all rain ceremonies. It is the most vital hereditary possession of the San Ildefonso people, linking Powhoge, Perage, and Otowi in unbroken continuity.

Two types of excavated cliff dwellings are found at Otowi. The first is the open-front dwelling (Fig. 25h ), usually, though not always, single-chambered—in most cases a natural cave, enlarged and shaped by excavation. The second is wholly artificial (Fig. 25c) with closed front of the natural rock *in situ*. These are usually multiple-chambered with floors below the level of the threshold; generally a crude fireplace beside the doorway, seldom provided with smoke vent; rooms usually rectangular and well shaped; floors plastered always, and walls usually plastered to a height of three or four feet. The front walls are from one to two feet thick. In some cases a little masonry has been used for casing about the doorways. Occasionally, porches were built over doorways, but nowhere were there large house groups against the cliff as at Puyé and in the Rito. For the most part, the dwellings are found in clusters and at two levels, that is, at the top of long steep slopes of the talus and again in the face of a second terrace above.

My first work at Otowi was done under the auspices of the Smithsonian Institution. This occupied the excavating season of 1905, April to September. The results have been partially published in Bureau of American Ethnology and School of American Research reports. The collections obtained are mainly in the United States National Museum. I wish to acknowledge the generosity of the Smithsonian Institution in furnishing me, recently, with photographs of Otowi pottery, with permission to use them in this publication. Subsequent to my excavations at Otowi, Dr. L. L. W. Wilson, assisted by our curator of archaeology in the Museum of New Mexico, Mr. Wesley Bradfield, carried on the work from where I left off for two seasons, with excellent results. The collection from Dr. Wilson's excavations went to the Commercial Museum of Philadelphia. With especial gratitude I acknowledge the recent gift of this valuable collection to our institution in Santa Fe.

The excavations at Otowi have been mainly in the cemeteries. This site has been the most prolific in archaeological material of all that have been studied in the Rio Grande drainage. The main cemetery lay on the slope a few feet to the south of the buildings. The mound was oblong, having a long diameter of about one hundred feet and a short diameter of about eighty feet. It was composed of black soil, the greater part of which must have been brought from the valley. The floor of the mound was the light gray tufa in place. This mound was excavated and may be taken as a type of prehistoric burial places of the Tewa.

Beginning at the perimeter of the mound on the west side, a trench ten feet wide was carried through the center, the earth being removed to the floor. The first interment was encountered at twelve feet from the edge of the mound at a depth of three feet. At fifteen feet burials became numerous and continued so for approximately thirty feet, after which they became less numerous and disappeared entirely before the east side of the mound was reached. Some forty skeletons were uncovered in the digging of this trench. The mound was then opened through the center by another ten-foot trench at right angles with the first, after which the remaining sectors were cleared. About fifteen thousand cubic feet of earth was moved in the examination of this mound. The number of interments could not be determined exactly, owing to the confused arrangement of the skeletal remains, caused by the disturbance of early burials to make room for later ones. The number was approximately one hundred and fifty. Of these, considerable portions of eighty were saved for transportation to the National Museum. Parts of about twenty more, in such a state of confusion that they could not be related in the field, were also sent. The remainder were decomposed. Nearly 20 per cent of the skeletal remains were those of infants. There was an appreciable number of secondary burials (Figs. 68 and 69). The soil of the mound increased in depth from three feet at the rim to six feet at the center. Burials were most numerous at a depth of three and of six feet, but were found at all levels from six inches below the surface to the bottom of the mound. A few were found in the rock floor. To accommodate these, small oblong pits about twelve inches deep and fifteen inches wide by three feet long had been dug. These evidently were the earliest interments.

A smaller cemetery a few feet west of the buildings was also excavated. It was a circular mound about thirty feet in diameter. The soil was from one to three feet deep. It was on sloping ground, and to prevent the washing away of the soil, a retaining wall about three feet high had been built around the lower rim. This was constructed of irregular pieces of tufa, piled rather than laid. This mound contained twenty-five interments, seven being infants. The excavation was conducted as in the larger mound.

No uniform burial position was found in the cemeteries. The skeletons were disposed in almost every possible reclining position except full length, which was never found to occur in ancient Tewa mounds. At Otowi, more were placed upon the back than upon the face or side, while at other places excavated in the same region the majority were face downward. In all cases, the knees were drawn up against the thorax. In some cases, a coarse matting was found covering the face, occasionally plastered over with clay. In a few burials, fragments of basketry were found about the head (Fig. 28). In many instances, the neck and loins were wrapped with cotton cord. The custom of burying pottery with the dead was practically invariable.

Generally used for this purpose were food bowls (Fig. 47), which were of all sizes from four to sixteen inches in diameter. Their contents had been perishable material, only meal and corncobs being distinguishable. Animal bones were numerous in the mound, but were never found in the food bowls. In only a few cases were water jars used for mortuary purposes; neither was it customary to use cooking utensils for this purpose, though a few were found. The custom of breaking the pottery at burial was prevalent, probably 50 per cent having been so treated.

Bone awls and pottery polishing stones were abundant. A few specimens of a fife-like instrument of turkey bone were found. Ceremonial pipes, in all cases the straight tube, more correctly named "cloud blowers," were occasionally found, usually upon the pelvis of the skeleton. These were mostly of clay, some of stone. One, made of ribbon onyx, is a very beautiful specimen of primitive art. There is notable rarity of projectile points, stone axes, or other implements for use in war, except sling stones—small spherical balls of agate.

The pottery obtained consists mainly of food bowls. Little is found in the houses, due probably to its having been carried away by the inhabitants on making their short migration to the valley. From the cemeteries came a very large collection, the greater part of which may be seen in the National Museum and in the Museum of New Mexico. It consists of a small amount of corrugated and indented ware, mostly fragmentary when found, used mainly in cooking vessels; some smooth undecorated ware, mostly small bird forms; a small number of pieces decorated by incision; and a large number with painted and glazed decoration, comprising at least 75 per cent of all the specimens found. The latter, as before mentioned, were principally food bowls, in nearly all cases having both interior and exterior decoration. The clay used was not of first-rate quality. It contained a considerable amount of fine sand and the product was rather porous, quite thick and heavy. Exceptions to this are found, in which a finer clay was obtained and prepared, making an excellent paste and permitting the fabrication of fine, thin ware.

These aboriginal potters had an accurate knowledge of colors. Gray ware was always decorated with black lines; red ware had,

Fig. 68.  Secondary Burial at Otowi

Fig. 69.  Another Secondary Burial at Otowi

FIG. 70. THE OLD NIGHT DANCE OF TYÚONYI (BY AWA-TSIREH)

almost invariably, a translucent glaze over the black lines. Several shades of red were used, two being often applied to the same bowl. The system of ornamentation was bold, striking, and, in execution, ranges from very crude to very good. Representative motives were sparingly used. No anthropomorphic designs were found. Zoömorphs were rare; the turtle, horned toad, and bird appear, unconventionalized. Bird and reptile designs, highly conventionalized, are numerous. In at least 90 per cent of all the decoration there is highly developed symbolism. Certain motives are very persistent, displaying many variants, but capable of being reduced to a few fundamental conceptions.

Our excavations at Sankewi'i and Tsirege were devoted to the great community buildings, the burial places, and to the small outlying ruins scattered over the adjacent mesas. The latter exist in large numbers. Our work laid bare enough of them to establish the fact that they are older than the great community houses. They appear to have been homes of from one to a dozen families each. The indications are that their inhabitants eventually merged to form the large communities. It is probable that they are remnants of Pajaritan people of an early epoch, when families and clans lived to themselves.

Sufficient excavating was done at the large ruins, Sankewi'i and Tsirege, to disclose their approximate ground plans. At Sankewi'i is seen the usual quadrangular arrangement of four buildings. The cemeteries lie just outside the court at the open corners. Tsirege is shown by a restoration which is as faithful a representation of the community buildings as could be made without excavating the entire ruin (Fig. 15). The restoration shows the outline of the mesa on which the ruin is situated, the location of the cliff houses, distribution of ceremonial chambers, and the trails by which the town was approached. The large pueblos were four stories high and may have contained from 1,200 to 1,500 rooms. There were probably no exterior doorways on the ground floor, each story being reached by ladders which could be drawn up when not in use.

We excavated the main cemetery at nearby Sankewi'i and, in addition, two small burial mounds. These were similar to the small mound at Otowi. A description of the method of work and material obtained would be a repetition of what has already been said. Forty skeletons were obtained from the two small mounds, thirty-two from the main cemetery. A considerable amount of pottery and other artifacts, not differing materially from the Otowi collections, was uncovered.

The skeletal remains from Sankewi'i and Tsirege were sent to the National Museum and have been studied and reported upon by Dr. Hrdlička. The pottery and other artifacts are herewith illustrated along with material from Puyé, Otowi, El Rito de los Frijoles, and minor excavations.

In the burial places of the villages above named, five modes of disposing of the dead were found: namely, in narrow chambers within the houses, under the fireplaces in living-rooms, in urns, in crypts, and in cemeteries. In all, the embryonic position prevailed, that is, with the knees drawn up against the chest. Any other burial position is almost unknown in the Pueblo region. Burial at full length was introduced with Christianity, though it has been found in a few localities that are obviously pre-Spanish. In intermural burial, the dead were left in long narrow chambers in a sitting posture, accompanied by food bowls and domestic utensils. This was not common. The fireplace burials were those of children. After a burial, the fireplace was plastered over and abandoned. At Puyé we found infant and fetal burials in small vessels which were usually covered with large food bowls, then placed in a corner of a room and covered with clay. We found at Otowi the bones of adults, disjointed and disposed in large food bowls, the skull being placed on top. Again, the bones were disjointed, laid side by side, the skull upon them with food bowl inverted over it, and this, in turn, covered with larger bowls until four or five had been used to cover the bones (Figs. 68 and 69). These were, of course, secondary interments. Probably they were first intermural burials, and when the bones had fallen apart they were gathered up and placed in the cemeteries.

Crypt or cave burial was here secondary. Mortuary crypts were posterior chambers to pueblo-like cliff dwellings. They were receptacles for great quantities of disjointed bones, the rooms being filled with these unrelated remains to a depth of several feet. No utensils accompanied them. I consider these crypts to have been depositaries for bones removed from, or washed out of, the cemeteries above. In individual cave burial as practiced in this region the dead are found in embryonic position and usually wrapped in feather robes or matting of yucca fiber.

In no other mound excavations in the Rio Grande Valley have I found any form of urn burial, unless the practice of inverting the food bowl over the head may be considered a survival of that custom. This was common at Otowi, Tsirege, and Sankewi'i. At Otowi, true urn burials were found. Two forms of the custom were observed, both evidently secondary burials. In one, the bowl was filled with small bones, meal, and wrappings of matting and cord. The long bones were disposed within the bowl, the ends protruding and the skull resting on top of all. In another case the skull was covered with matting, prepared clay, and ashes. Over this was placed about half of a broken food bowl. On and about this were disposed the small bones. The long bones were adjusted about the head. Over all a large bowl was inverted, the ends of the long bones protruding from beneath. One infant skeleton was found at Otowi with a small bowl beside it, under a large inverted bowl which entirely covered it. No traces of incineration were seen, though the majority of burials were accompanied by quantities of ashes and charcoal, pointing to a prevalent custom of making funerary fires.

The cemeteries lie just outside the courts and consist of mounds that measure from fifty to one hundred feet in diameter. In some cases the earth had to be brought from a distance, as no soil existed on the summit of the rocky plateau. In some instances the capacity of the mound was increased by the addition of a second layer of earth after the first stratum was filled. The number of interments in the cemeteries seem to bear little relation to the population of the village. One mound at Tsirege contained about one hundred, one at Sankewi'i forty, and one at Otowi one hundred and twenty-five. I suspect that the remains were not long respected—that they were soon disturbed by new burials, also exposed by the rains in flood season and then transferred to the crypts below.

APPENDICES

# List of Illustrations

## Appendix I

# PAJARITAN PICTOGRAPHY

## THE CAVE PICTOGRAPHS OF THE RITO DE LOS FRIJOLES

### *By* KENNETH M. CHAPMAN

HE PAJARITO PLATEAU of northern New Mexico is a particularly rich field for the study of petroglyphs, for, in the neighborhood of the more important ruins of communal buildings, the sheer cliffs of soft volcanic tuff offered many flat surfaces to encourage the art of picture writing. Such pictographs have been described in works upon the archaeology of this region, but so far no mention has been made of the occurrence of a different class of drawings found upon the smoke blackened, clay plastered walls of cave dwellings. Many such had been noted in the course of studies by the School of American Research, between the years 1909 and 1914, though the several seasons of excavation gave no opportunity for a systematic study of these more obscure records of an early period.

In August, 1915, however, a party headed by the late Mr. Frank Springer, then a member of the Board of Regents of the School, found on examining a few of the cave dwellings of the Rito de los Frijoles that some of the most valuable of these drawings were in danger of being obliterated by the elements, and by mutilation at the hands of vandal tourists whose activity was everywhere manifest. To the late Carlos Vierra, a member of the party, is due the greatest credit for having called attention to some recent vandalism, and for having volunteered to assist in a survey of the entire cave group. The proposed work was generously approved by Mr. Springer even though he saw the well planned vacation for his party suddenly transformed into an intensive project for two, and at times three of its members. With the author, Mr. Vierra gave freely of his time during the remainder of the month, and renewed his coöperation during August of 1916. The survey, then nearly finished, was finally brought to completion by the author during the summer of 1920.

The typical excavated cave dwellings of the Pajarito Plateau are entered by small doorways hewn into the face of the cliff. The caves are usually rectangular in form and average about seven by nine feet

FIG. 1.  HUNTER AND DEER

in size. The floors and the walls, to a height of three or four feet, are smoothly plastered with clay. Each cave contains a fireplace in a front corner. A draught was induced by a vent through the face of the cliff, either above or beside the doorway. The ventilation thus produced must have been far from satisfactory for both ceiling and plastered walls soon become blackened by smoke. The ceilings were left untouched but the smoothly plastered walls were frequently freshened by the application of a thin wash of clay. As many as twenty of these superimposed layers have been found on some of the cave walls, each showing that it had become entirely blackened by smoke before it had been covered by a fresh coat.

Only a few of the dwellings have withstood the ravages of time. Many have been damaged by the seepage of water through ever widening fissures in the cliffs, while the fronts of others have fallen out, exposing the side and rear walls to the action of wind and rain, until, in many instances, but a hand's breadth of plaster adhering to the eroded surface of the cliff tells the tale of a former dwelling.

The abandonment of the entire Pajarito Plateau is assumed to have taken place prior to the coming of Coronado into New Mexico, in 1540. If refuge was sought in the canyon of the Rito de los Frijoles by considerable groups from the Rio Grande pueblos at any time after the arrival of the Spaniards, no recognizable trace of their occupation has been revealed by the extensive excavations in the ruins of the circular house of Tyúonyi and the adjacent talus groups, or by the presence of pottery types known to have been developed after the close of the seventeenth century. It seems safe, therefore, to assume that with the exception of a small group of dwellings known to have been occupied by a Spanish-speaking family during the past one hundred years, the majority of the caves of the Rito de los Frijoles have not been used as permanent homes since pre-Spanish times.

FIG. 2. PENCIL RUBBING OF A MASK DESIGN

In the examination of pictographs upon the walls of several hundred such caves, it became necessary to distinguish between the pre-Spanish and the recent, as there were many drawings evidently done by vandals and sheep herders. The Pueblo Indians, employed by the School for several seasons in the nearby excavations, have also left examples of their handiwork in several caves occupied by them, and many of these might have been confused with the work of the ancient Pajaritans were it not for the freshness of their appearance. Another class of work of more doubtful antiquity consists of petroglyphs crudely hewn or pecked into the blackened ceilings or walls of a few of the caves. The fact that these were usually unblackened by smoke seems to point to their having been done since the abandonment of the group.  But an unquestioned antiquity must be accorded to incised drawings upon the plastered walls, whose lines are completely blackened by smoke, and to others which are partly covered by adhering particles of many successive coats of clay.

FIG. 3.  SUPERIMPOSED DRAWINGS OF DETAILS OF BIRDS

In several instances the drawings could be copied by photography (Plates I and II).  But by far the greater number were so blackened by the subsequent smoking that they could be recovered only by pencil rubbings, from which pen drawings were then made.  (Compare Fig. 2 with Plate XII, *f*).  The use of a flash lamp revealed many drawings in dark corners which would otherwise have escaped attention.  In addition, fifteen excellent plasticine impressions were made from the more remarkable drawings, the plaster casts of which give exact reproductions of the originals. By these various means over two hundred copies were secured, of which a total of 125 are here reproduced. Included for comparison are three drawings from similar cave dwellings at Puyé (Plates IV, *h;* VI, *d;* and XV, *f*). In preparing the plates for reproduction it has been found advisable to reduce the relative size of certain drawings by photography. In general it may be said that most of the figures are approximately one-eighth to one-tenth natural size. As constant blackening of the walls obliterated

FIG. 4. PICTOGRAPHS SCRATCHED ON A CAVE WALL

many of the drawings, the cave dwellers had used the same surface for other figures. Thus the pencil rubbings revealed numerous examples as complex as the group in Fig. 3.

The drawings showing evidence of pre-Spanish origin include a wide range of subjects, from apparently the crude and meaningless scrawls of children to figures which reveal the skill of a practiced hand. The subjects may be broadly classified as geometric designs, symbolic devices, and human, animal, and bird figures.

Thirty-five geometric figures were copied. Typical examples are reproduced in Plates III and IV. Many of these are elongated bands, filled with terraced, crooked, and zigzag designs, suggestive of textile or ceramic patterns.

The art of the entire Pueblo area is and always has been a highly stylized one, developed largely through the technique of textile and

ceramic designs. Hence in the representation of certain supernatural attributes of man or animals, the use of symbolic devices
derived mainly from a geometric art was of greater importance than
the lifelike portrait of the subject. This conventional treatment is
apparent in most of the pictographs of life forms.

FIG. 5. GROUP OF HUNTERS AT
LEFT OF THE LARGE GROUP
IN FIG. 6

The bird was a favorite decorative
motive with the ancient Pajaritans as is
shown by thirty-six drawings, ranging
from fairly realistic forms to others which
could not be recognized as birds, or parts
of birds, if it were not for certain symbolic
features found in the entire series. A certain degree of realism is expressed in the
bird figures in Plate VI. But, in most of
the others, it is evident that the artists
were more concerned with recording their

FIG. 6.  HUNTERS AND DEER

interpretations of mythical creatures possessing other attributes in no
way related to known bird forms. The formal head plumage, the
exaggerated curve of elongated beaks, and other features are quite
unlike those of bird forms used in their contemporary pottery decoration. But the stepped device in the headdress of Plate VIII, *b*, and
between the wing and body of *e*, shown enlarged in *f*, dates the drawings as pre-Spanish or early post-Spanish, for this symbol of the eagle
tail feather is known to have been discarded from Pueblo ceramic
decoration at an early period. A study of the decorative or symbolic
details of many of the other figures leads to the conclusion that a bird
is also the theme of the complex drawing in Plate X, *g*. In this the
headdress is identical with that on the human figure in Plate XI, *d*.

The human figures are usually very sketchily outlined drawings of katsinas, or supernatural beings which are still impersonated by masked dancers in some of the Rio Grande pueblos, but now principally in ceremonies at Zuñi and the Hopi pueblos (Plates I, II, XI, XII, XIII). For these the front view is most commonly used, both in drawings of the entire figure and for the representation of the masks alone. The concept of the features of a face within a hand, in Plate XI, *f,* is unusual in Pueblo art.

Quite unlike the drawings of katsinas, are four examples of human figures, singly and in groups, associated with animals in hunting scenes. These are such a departure from the usual conventional representations of masked dancers that their genuineness as drawings of the early period might well be questioned. But a careful examination of the character of the smoke-blackened walls on which they

FIG. 6. *(Continued)*

appear leads to the conclusion that they are authentic examples of a theme contemporaneous with the other drawings of the early period. The action of some of the figures is in no way remarkable (Plate I, *a* and Fig. 4), but that of the single hunter in Fig. 1 is quite realistic as compared with the more formal style of a much later period. Even more action is found in the twelve hunters shown in Figs. 5 and 6. Although sketchily scratched on an unusually rough plastered surface, they show a considerable knowledge of action. The crouching posture of several figures and the lifelike stance of the hunter with drawn bow make this a most remarkable group.

Mammals appear but rarely in the cave drawings. Except for those in the hunting scenes, only two were found in condition to be copied (Fig. 7). In these, as with many of the drawings of birds, the artists have apparently made no serious attempt at realism. The deer and faun in Fig. 6 are equally crude, but the drawing of the squirrel

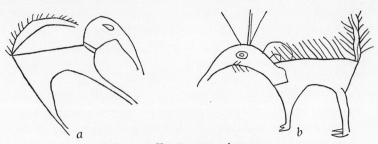

FIG. 7.   UNIDENTIFIED ANIMALS

FIG. 8.   MOUNTAIN SHEEP

(Plate II, *b*) and of two of the deer in the hunting scene (Fig. 1) shows a remarkable departure from the conventions of the all-pervading geometric art of early Pueblo times. In the latter, the drawing of the hind quarter of the doe at the right, done with simplicity and assurance, is comparable with that of a mountain sheep (Fig. 8) which is, perhaps, the most remarkably realistic of all the animal figures recovered thus far in the Southwest. The incurved horn brought forward across the neck suggests a deliberate attempt at three dimensional drawing in simple outlines.

Less numerous and easily distinguishable from the ancient drawings of men and animals are those of a period long after the abandonment of the caves, when occasional wayfarers left their crude attempts

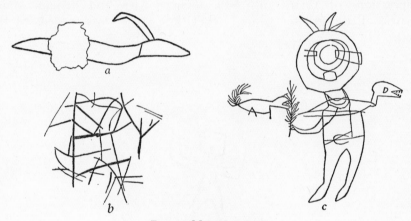

FIG. 9. MISCELLANEOUS

at picturing a horse and rider (Plate XV), a subject which identifies the work definitely as post-Spanish. Of an equally late period also are examples of the Christian cross and other symbols left by native New Mexican herders and hunters. Among these is a crude copy of a religious painting (Plate XIV, *d*), the features of which are done in a style quite unlike that of the Pueblo Indians. Other drawings, such as the mask and the cloud and rain symbol (Plate XIV, *e* and *g*) are more commonly found in a comparatively late period of Pueblo art, though their exact position in the sequence of the cave drawings cannot be determined.

A few of the larger caves, once used as kivas, contain remnants of mural painting in many colors, which must have been comparable with the best of those recovered in recent years by the University of

New Mexico at Kuaua, and by the Peabody Museum at Awatovi. Compared with such finished work, the incised drawings from the cave dwellings of the Rito de los Frijoles are seen to be mere rough sketches, done by aid of the dim and flickering light of fireplaces in the homes. Unhampered by the laborious process of hewing or pecking line after line deep into the surface of the cliffs, or by the more formal requirements of textile or pottery decoration, the ancient cliff dwellers here recorded in a few seconds, or in a few minutes at the most, impressions of their daily life, their fancies and beliefs, which possess all the greater value in that they are artless records of the past.

PLATE I

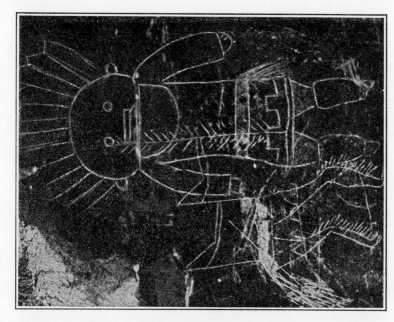

PICTOGRAPHS OF KATSINAS FROM CAVE WALL

PLATE II

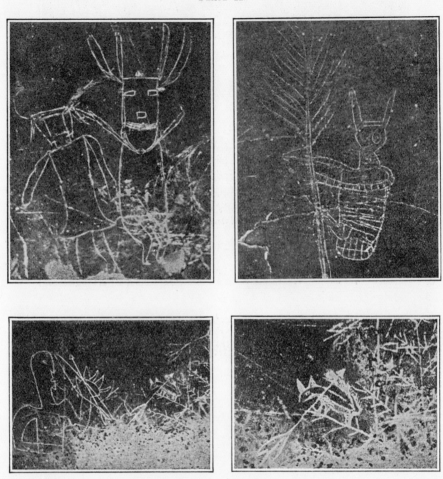

PICTOGRAPHS FROM CAVE WALLS

PLATE III

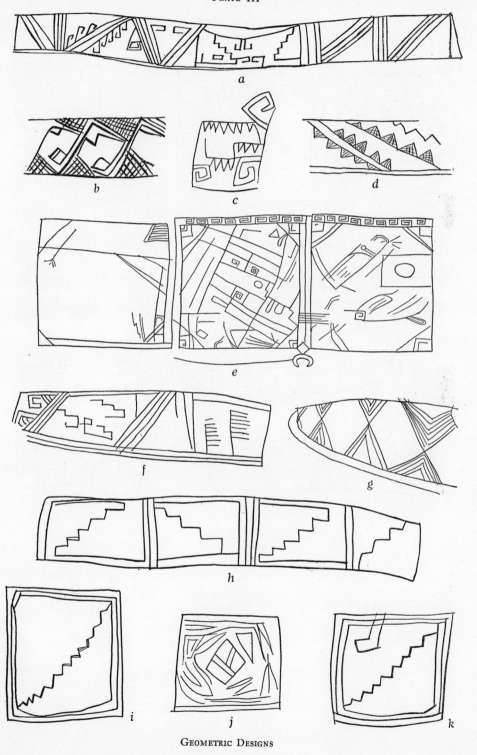

GEOMETRIC DESIGNS

PLATE IV

TERRACES AND OTHER GEOMETRIC DESIGNS

PLATE V

GEOMETRIC DESIGNS

PLATE VI

BIRDS OF REALISTIC FORM

PLATE VII

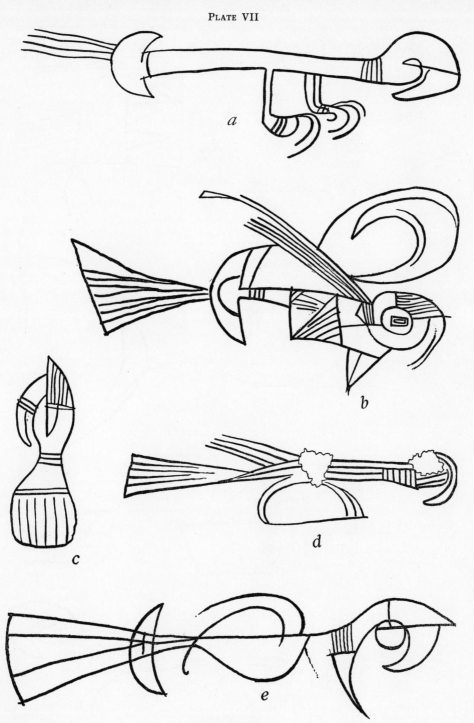

*a*

*b*

*c*

*d*

*e*

STYLIZED BIRDS

PLATE VIII

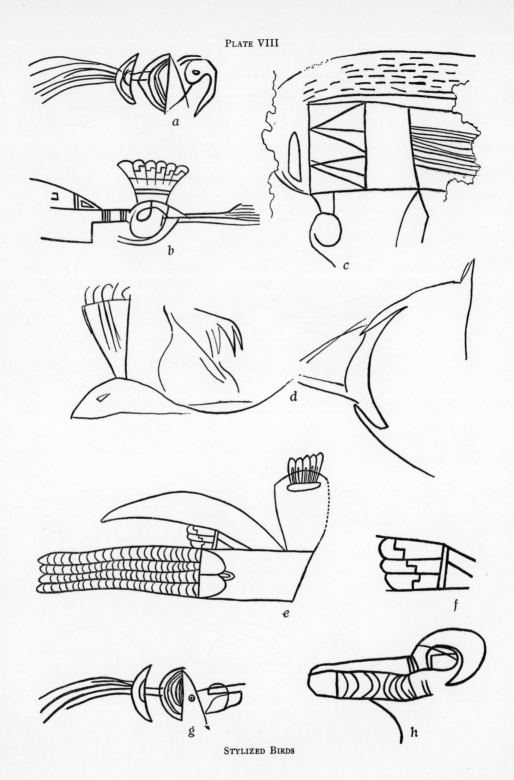

STYLIZED BIRDS

PLATE IX

STYLIZED BIRDS

PLATE X

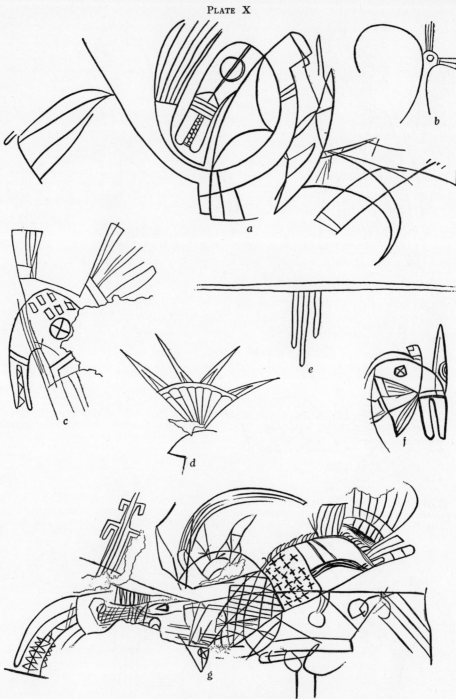

MORE COMPLEX STYLIZED BIRDS

Plate XI

THE HUMAN FIGURE IN PROFILE AND IN FRONT VIEW

PLATE XII

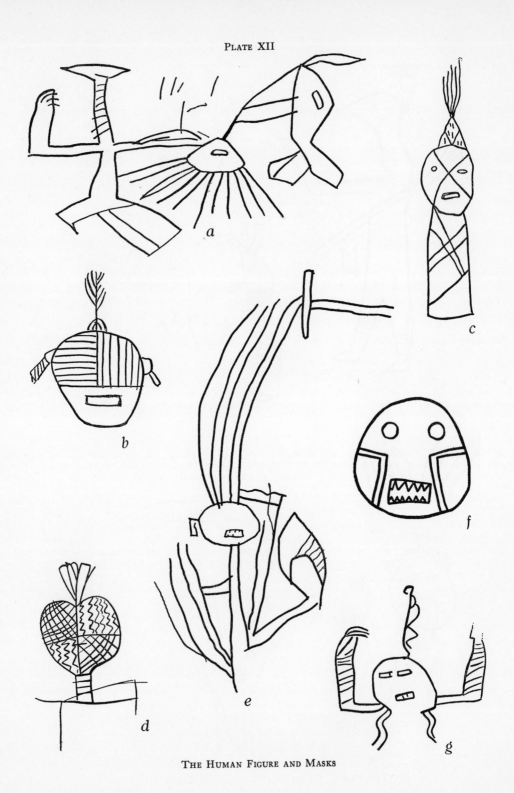

THE HUMAN FIGURE AND MASKS

PLATE XIII

THE HUMAN FIGURE AND MASKS

PLATE XIV

MISCELLANEOUS PICTOGRAPHS

PLATE XV

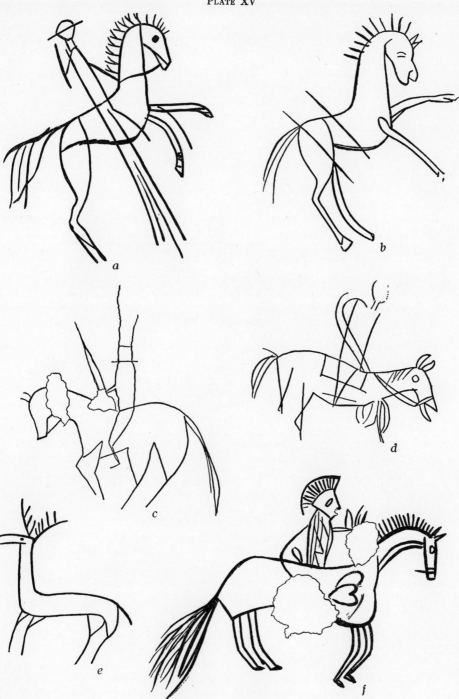

PICTOGRAPHS OF A RECENT PERIOD

# FROM THE ARCHIVES

*By* Sylvanus G. Morley

## The Rito de los Frijoles in the Spanish Archives

The earliest mention, in Spanish documents, of the region in which lies the canyon known today as the Rito de los Frijoles, is in the will of one Andres Montoya, dated at Santa Fe, New Mexico, June 17, 1740. This document says, in part, describing a piece of property owned by the testator, "and the other, on the other side of the Rito del Norte, which I have not put into cultivation because of my infirmities, which is situate between the fields of the Pueblos of San Ildefonso and Cochiti, the boundaries of said tract being distant from one and the other pueblos half a league." The tract of land thus described would necessarily include within its confines the Rito de los Frijoles, although no mention of such a name is made in the Montoya will.

Two years later, under date of March 20, 1742, at Santa Fe, one Pedro Sanchez petitions the then governor of the province of New Mexico, Don Gaspar Domingo de Mendosa, that he be permitted to register for a piece of property, which he describes as follows: "a piece of land on the other side of the river Del Norte uncultivated and abandoned, and as such unoccupied, there being no one having any claim thereto, the boundaries being, on the north the lands enjoyed by the Indians of the Pueblo of San Ildefonso; on the south the lands of Captain Andres Montoya; on the east the Del Norte river and on the west the Rocky Mountains." This petition of Pedro Sanchez was acted upon favorably by Governor Mendosa, and the tract of land above described was given to him. This grant was acquired from the heirs of Sanchez by Ramon Vigil, under whose name the tract is now known.

The first of these two early instruments, the Montoya will, shows that, at some time prior to 1740, a tract of land including the present canyon of the Rito de los Frijoles was given to one Andres Montoya, who further states that he had not, up to the year 1740, put this property under cultivation, and we may conclude, consequently, that it was up to that time unbroken land. The Sanchez petition further corroborates the Montoya will by stating two years later that the Montoya lands bound the Sanchez tract on the south.

The next mentions of this region are in three original documents dating from 1803, 1807, and 1814, filed as Exhibits B, C, and A, respectively, in the papers of the Rito de los Frijoles land grant in the Surveyor General's office at Santa Fe. Exhibit C, although dating from 1807, four years after the writing of Exhibit B, deals with a time earlier than Exhibit B and, consequently, should be examined first, in order that the chronological sequence of events may be preserved.

Exhibit C was written at Santa Fe, New Mexico, under date of December 28, 1807, by one Father Antonio Cavallero, a Franciscan in charge of the mission at Cochiti. It is a certificate of events which the Father knew to have happened in the year 1780 at Cochiti, which had a bearing upon the tract of land now mentioned for the first time in this instrument as the Rito de los Frijoles.

The Father certified that in the year 1780 the then governor of the province of New Mexico, Colonel Juan Bautista de Anza, made a judicial visit to Cochiti; that during the course of this visit one Andres Montoya (the testator in the will above mentioned) appeared before the governor and requested him to look over a grant made to him, Montoya, of the tract called the Rito de los Frijoles by a former governor of the province, Don Tomas Viles Cachupin.

The Father further certified that Montoya stated that he had held this tract without improving it or even breaking the land up to that time, until he had become so enfeebled by age he was no longer able to accomplish such an undertaking, and that, moreover, he lacked the necessary means so to do; consequently, for these reasons, he begged the governor to convey his title to the land in question to his son-in-law, Juan Antonio Lujan. Father Cavallero further certified that Governor Anza made this transfer of title and that, thereupon, "said Lujan commenced to work said farm in which he labored very much in clearing it off, it being virgin land." The certificate concludes with Father Cavallero's statement that one Jose Antonio Salas, the son-in-law of the Juan Antonio Lujan above mentioned, had appeared before him and requested him to write out these facts which had come under his personal notice, and since he (Father Cavallero) could not well refuse such a just and reasonable request he had written out these things which he knew to be true since they happened before his eyes.

This certificate of Father Cavallero's is important because of two facts which it establishes about the region in question:

(1) That this region had received the name Rito de los Frijoles some time prior to the year 1780, when Governor de Anza made a judicial visit to Cochiti.

(2) That the region known as the Rito de los Frijoles remained unbroken and "virgin land" up to the year 1780.

The next documentary notice of this region is Exhibit B above mentioned, which, although written four years earlier than the Cavallero certificate, treats of matters contemporaneous with its writing and does not deal with events in the eighteenth century as did Exhibit C.

Exhibit B is a petition under date of February 28, 1803, addressed at Santa Fe, to the then governor of the province of New Mexico, Don Jose Manrique, by Jose Antonio Salas, the same man who solicited the certificate of Father Cavallero given above as Exhibit C. He petitions, "that whereas I have lost the grant of a farm, which I possess, called the Rito de los Frijoles, given by Governor Juan Bautista de Anza, the original of which is found in the archives of the government . . . I earnestly entreat that said original may be delivered to me."

Exhibits B and C fit together very nicely. It seems that some time between the years 1780 and 1803 the original grant to the tract, known as the Rito de los Frijoles, was either lost or destroyed. In 1803, the owner of the property was Jose Antonio Salas, who acquired his right through marriage with Antonia Rosa Lujan, the daughter of Juan Antonio Lujan, who was the son-in-law of the original grantee, Andres Montoya. In 1803, this Jose Antonio Salas evidently thought it best to get the original grant to this property from the archives in Santa Fe, perhaps to fortify his wife's right to this tract. To this end he addressed a petition (Exhibit B) to Governor Manrique, asking to have the original paper deposited with him, binding himself to produce the same in court whenever required so to do. Evidently this request was not granted, or the copy in the archives was lost, for, in 1807, this same Jose Antonio Salas asked the priest at Cochiti to write out a certificate which would show his wife's right to the land. This the priest at Cochiti, Father Cavallero, did (Exhibit C).

The final notice of the Rito de los Frijoles in the Spanish documents appears in Exhibit A, above mentioned. This document consists of four parts, dated April 1, 2, 3, and 4, 1814, respectively. The first part, under date of April 1, 1814, is a petition addressed at Santa Fe to the then governor of New Mexico, Don Jose Manrique, by Antonia Rosa Lujan y Salas, the widow of Jose Antonio Salas, mentioned in Exhibits B and C, in which she begs permission to be allowed to return to the grant made to her grandfather, Andres Montoya, deceased, which she was obliged to vacate in 1811 for reasons given in her petition as follows: "On account of some robberies having occurred, committed by other indifferent persons who had banded themselves together to live there," i. e., at the Rito de los Frijoles. The second part, dated the following day, is Governor Manrique's delegation of authority to a citizen of Santa Fe, one Antonio Ortiz, to proceed in the matter for him. The governor states further why his petitioner and others had been ordered to vacate this region in 1811 more fully than Antonia Rosa Lujan's account in Part 1: "Because of their evil deeds, and not finding amongst them any formality in defensive improvements in that place such as houses, and other things required of settlers, on the contrary that they lived in caves the same as barbarians." The following day, April 3, 1814, Antonio Ortiz filed his report. He states that Antonia Rosa Lujan gave him, as evidence of her right to this tract, a document (Exhibit C above) which he deemed insufficient, and required further proof. Whereupon one Mariano Romero, a lieutenant of militia, was brought before him, who testified, in substance, as follows: That when Juan Antonio Lujan, the petitioner's father, had commenced the clearing and breaking of the land, he claimed that two brothers, Domingo and Miguel Romero, appeared and contested his right to the property on the grounds that it belonged to the heirs of Andres Montoya. Subsequently, the Romero brothers became partners with Juan Antonio Lujan, being related to him through his wife, and their objections were withdrawn, and the family of Antonia Rosa Lujan, who married Jose Antonio Salas, lived in undisputed possession of the property up to the year 1811. Ortiz concludes his report by referring the matter for final settlement back to Governor Manrique.

The last part of Exhibit A is dated April 4, 1814, and is Governor Manrique's final decision in the matter. He allows Antonia Rosa Lujan to return to the Rito de los Frijoles and reoccupy that region on her promise of good conduct. He stipulates further that she shall not harbor questionable characters, nor shelter cattle thieves, whose misdemeanors have been notorious in the district to which she is returning. Finally, that if she depart from good conduct in any of these matters she will be prosecuted to the full extent of the law.

Exhibit A is interesting chiefly because, in Part 2, for the first time in the Spanish documents, reference is made to the cliff dwellings of the Rito de los Frijoles. They are here described as caves like those lived in by the barbarians. Another point of interest established by Parts 1, 2, and 4, of this document, is that in the early part of the nineteenth century, Rito de los Frijoles was the haunt of a robber band, the depredations of which became so troublesome to the people living in and around Santa Fe, that, in the year 1811, all inhabitants of the Rito de los Frijoles tract were ordered to vacate it and move elsewhere.

After the return of Antonia Rosa Lujan to the region, in 1814, her descendants seem to have occupied the region continuously except when driven out temporarily by attacks of marauding Indians, probably the Navajos, down to the present time.

On March 14, 1883, Exhibits A, B, and C were approved by Henry M. Atkinson, United States Surveyor General, and were by him forwarded to Congress for final action. Congress having failed to act in this matter, it came before the Court of Private Land Claims which, on September 27, 1894, rejected the claim of the Lujan heirs and assignees and dismissed their petition. An appeal was taken to the United States Supreme Court, which body sustained the decision of the lower court on December 9, 1895.

The question of the boundaries of the so-called Rito de los Frijoles grant was always somewhat in dispute because of the loss of the original granting paper. The consensus of opinion seems to have been that the grant was bounded on the north by the Cañada Ancha and the Potrero de Pajarito, on the east by the Rio Grande, on the south by the edge of the Cañada del Alamo, and on the west by the Valles (Jemez) Mountains. The dismissal of the petition to have the Rito de los Frijoles grant approved by the Court of Private Land Claims, by both the Court of Private Land Claims and the Supreme Court of the United States, of course, did away with that grant. The Ramon Vigil grant, the grant next north of the Rito de los Frijoles grant, was extended by this decision southward to the northern edge of the Rito de los Frijoles canyon; and the grant of the Cochiti Indians, the next grant on the south of the Rito de los Frijoles grant, was thereby extended northward to the southern boundary of the Ramon Vigil grant.

## PRESERVATION OF AMERICAN ANTIQUITIES*

### GOVERNMENT SUPERVISION OF HISTORIC AND PREHISTORIC RUINS [1]

The traffic in prehistoric wares from the Southwest that has arisen during the past few years, with the attendant destruction of prehistoric remains, has become a matter of great concern to archeologists, who appreciate the gravity of this loss to anthropological science. Even though much of this material gathered by parties who are only commercially interested in it, eventually finds its way into public museums, its value to science is greatly reduced because of the absence of authentic records. Fortunately, a growing popular and educational interest in historic and prehistoric landmarks has arisen to assist in the preservation of these objects.

As a citizen of New Mexico who has watched with deep concern the loss of many of the incomparable archeological treasures of the Southwest, I have recently taken up in a more serious manner than ever before an inquiry into the question of how these monuments may be permanently preserved and prehistoric relics protected, at least long enough to permit of their scientific investigation. During the past few weeks, while pursuing certain lines of research at the national capital, for which the splendid resources of various government departments, bureaus, museums and libraries have been most courteously placed at my disposal, the opportunity has been given me to inform myself fully as to the care which the United States government has exercised over these ruins, is now exercising and stands ready to exercise whenever properly informed. The manifest desire to be informed, and the promptness with which information is digested and acted upon by the departments having jurisdiction over such matters are most encouraging.

*A reprint of some of the most important documents in the movement for the preservation of American antiquities which resulted in our present federal and state regulations.

[1] Reprinted from *Science,* n. s., Vol. XX, No. 517, Nov. 25, 1904, pp. 722-727.

In view of the fact that scientific bodies have come to take a commendable interest in this subject, and that various measures looking toward the protection and preservation of our prehistoric ruins have been and now are under consideration and may be brought before the national Congress next winter, it will be helpful in considering such measures to know that a wise and vigorous policy has been developed in the Department of the Interior with reference thereto. This policy, if vigorously pursued, practically accomplishes the ends to be desired and renders legislation of secondary importance. The following correspondence explains itself. I give, first, excerpts from a letter from the Honorable W. A. Richards, Commissioner of the General Land Office, under date of October 5, 1904.

Professor Edgar L. Hewett,
    Washington, D. C.

Sir: I beg to acknowledge the receipt of your letter of September 3, 1904, transmitting a memorandum relative to the historic and prehistoric ruins in Arizona, New Mexico, Colorado and Utah, and, also, of your letter, under date of September 14, 1904, in relation to proposed legislation for the protection of such ruins.

\*        \*        \*        \*

This office fully appreciates the necessity for protecting these ruins and the importance of furthering in every way possible, researches in connection therewith which are undertaken for the benefit of recognized scientific and educational institutions, with a view to increasing the knowledge of such objects and aiding in the general advancement of archaeological science; and it desires to aid all such efforts to the full extent of its power, while, at the same time, endeavoring to effectually protect the ruins and relics on the public lands from ruthless spoliation by parties plying a trade in such matters.

\*        \*        \*        \*

The need for adequate legislation on this subject has, accordingly, been called to the attention of congress by this department for a number of years, but as yet without avail.

In the meantime, every effort has been made to extend such protection to the various regions known to contain objects of interest as is possible without the requested legislation. Certain of the tracts have been protected from appropriation by being temporarily withdrawn from disposal under the public land laws. This action has been taken in the following cases:

In New Mexico: The Pajarito Cliff Dwellers' region, the Jemez Cliff Dwellers' region, the tract known as El Morro, or Inscription Rock.

In Colorado: The Mesa Verde Cliff Dwellers' region.

In Arizona: The tract containing the petrified forest; the greater portion of that part of the district designated by you as the Rio Verde district which lies outside of the Black Mesa Forest Reserve. This withdrawn area contains, among other ruins, the one known as Montezuma Castle.

\*      \*      \*      \*

As regards the regions which you mention as containing ruins of known importance, which fall within the boundaries of tracts that have been permanently set apart as forest reserves, or just outside of the boundaries thereof, you are advised that they are, in consequence, under the care of the forest force patrolling the reserves, and that instructions have, at different times, been issued to the forest officers in respect to having a general care of these ruins. Further and more specific instructions will now be given in regard to their care, based upon the information furnished by you.

The several regions thus under the supervision of the forest reserve force fall within the districts designated by you as follows:

In the Gila River Forest Reserve, New Mexico: The greater portions of both the Upper Gila District and the San Francisco River District.

In the Black Mesa Forest Reserve, Arizona: A portion of both the San Carlos District and the Rio Verde District; which latter contains what is known as Montezuma Well.

In the San Francisco Mountains Forest Reserve, Arizona: A portion of the Flagstaff District.

\*      \*      \*      \*

As yet, owing to the lack of sufficient available funds, it has not been practicable to place custodians in charge of the numerous and widely scattered ruins throughout the southwest, except in the case of three localities in Arizona. These cases are: The Casa Grande ruin; the Walnut Cañon ruins, lying partly within the San Francisco Mountains Forest Reserve; the ruins of Cañon del Muerto, within the Navajo Indian Reservation.

It is evident that immediate and effective measures should be taken by the government to protect regions containing objects of such great value to the ethnological history of this country and to other scientific studies;

\*      \*      \*      \*

I am also heartily in accord with your recommendation that, while many of the tracts containing ruins and other objects of interest need only to be temporarily withdrawn and protected until the ruins and objects thereon have been satisfactorily examined and utilized, yet, certain of the most important of these regions should be preserved permanently as national parks, and that a general law be enacted, authorizing the establishment of such parks, and making provision for their proper protection and management.

\*      \*      \*      \*

(Signed)    W. A. RICHARDS, *Commissioner.*

The following orders were sent out by the commissioner of the general land office a few days subsequent to the above correspondence:

Department of the Interior,
General Land Office, Washington, D. C.

Mr. F. S. Breen,                                    October 15, 1904.
Forest Supervisor,
Flagstaff, Arizona.

Sir: Your special attention is called to the historic and prehistoric ruins located in the San Francisco Mountains and Black Mesa Forest Reserves. As the ruins are almost entirely within said reserves, you are directed to exercise special care in their preservation. For your information in this matter I will state that there appears to be no special statute forbidding scientific research on the public lands, or requiring that permission shall be obtained before undertaking the same or removing objects of value from the public domain. At the same time, however, independent of positive legislative provision in the matter, the United Staes has all the civil remedies, whether for the prevention or redress of injuries, which individuals possess. And, since all unauthorized excavations upon public lands which tend to the injury of same or of ruins or relics thereon, or the removal of objects of value or of scientific or historic interest, are in the nature of trespass upon the lands, all such intrusion upon public lands renders the parties to the trespasses liable to prosecution.

It is, therefore, deemed advisable that all persons wishing to explore and make excavations of the ruins referred to, should secure permission from the department. This office appreciates the importance of aiding in every way possible all examinations and gatherings of objects of interest upon the public domain, which are undertaken for the benefit of recognized scientific and educational institutions, while, at the same time, endeavoring to effectually protect the ruins and dwellings on the public lands from ruthless spoliation by parties plying a trade in such matters.

You are hereby directed to use your best efforts to carry out the wishes of the department in this matter, and so instruct your subordinates.

Very respectfully,
(Signed)    W. A. RICHARDS, *Commissioner.*

Department of the Interior,
General Land Office, Washington, D. C.

Mr. Frank Grygla,                                    October 19, 1904.
    Special Agent, G. L. O.,
        Santa Fe, New Mexico.

Sir: Your special attention is called to the subject of the unauthorized explorations and excavations of the historic and prehistoric ruins located upon the public lands for purposes of traffic in the curios, relics, and objects of scientific and historic interest taken therefrom.

In order to prevent the further improvident spoliation and destruction of these ruins, and to restrict the explorations and excavations thereof to those made for the benefit of recognized scientific and educational institutions and objects, it is deemed advisable that all persons desiring to engage in such explorations shall secure permission therefor from the department before commencing their operations.

You will take prompt and appropriate measures to insure observance of the department's wishes with respect to such of said ruins as may be upon public lands, including those temporarily withdrawn with a view to the creation of forest reserves, or for other purposes, in your territory, and you will render all practicable assistance to the forest reserve and Indian offices in their efforts to protect the ruins upon the lands under their supervision from unauthorized explorations and excavations.

If in any instance adequate protection to the public interests in connection with these ruins cannot be obtained without recourse to legal proceedings, you will at once report the facts and the means of proving them to this office for consideration with a view to the institution of such proceedings.

Very respectfully,

(Signed)     W. A. RICHARDS, *Commissioner.*

Identical orders were sent to all forest supervisors and special agents of the General Land Office in the Southwest. These orders cover not less than three-fourths of all the ruins of New Mexico, Arizona, Colorado and Utah.

On or near all the important ruins that are situated on lands controlled by the General Land Office which have been withdrawn either permanently or temporarily the following notice, printed in conspicuous type on large sheets of tough white cloth, is kept posted by range riders and other officers:

WARNING:

*DEPARTMENT OF THE INTERIOR,*
GENERAL LAND OFFICE,
Washington, D. C.
May 24, 1904

Notice is hereby given that these lands have been withdrawn, for public purposes, from settlement, entry, and other disposal.

All persons are prohibited, under the penalty of the law, in such cases provided, from committing thereon any trespass whatever, and from working in any manner whatever any injury, waste, or damage of any kind to

these public lands and to the timber, natural curiosities, caves, ruins, objects
of antiquity, or any other public property thereon, and from removing or in
any way disturbing the same.

W. A. RICHARDS,
*Commissioner of the General Land Office.*

Approved: E. A. HITCHCOCK,
*Secretary of the Interior.*

The following excerpts from a letter from Hon. A. C. Tonner,
acting commissioner of Indian affairs, set forth the policy of that
department on the same subject:

Department of the Interior,
Office of Indian Affairs, Washington, D. C.

October 22, 1904.

Edgar L. Hewett, Esq.,
Washington, D. C.

Sir: This office is in receipt of your communication of the 17th instant,

\*      \*      \*      \*

In reply you are advised that this office has been and is fully alive to the
importance of preserving the various ruins and remains of antiquity scattered throughout the southwest, and has heretofore issued stringent orders
to many of the Indian officials in charge of the reservations to which you
refer—especially to those in charge of the Navajo, Moqui and Hualapi
reservations. Quite recently this office, in order to prevent the spoliation of
the prehistoric ruins in the cañons of De Chelly and Del Muerto, recommended to the secretary of the interior that a custodian be appointed to
have charge of the ruins in the said cañons, and authority was granted
by the secretary therefor and the custodian is now on duty.

In view of your present request the officials in charge of the various
Indian reservations to which you refer have, in letters of this day, been
advised relative to preventing further injury to ruins and suppressing the
traffic in prehistoric pottery which may be found on the reservations under
their care.

Their attention has been invited to the previous instructions of the office
relative to this matter and they have been requested to use their best
endeavors to keep out intruders and relic hunters and to see that such of the
remains of antiquity as may be located within the reserves under their
respective charges are kept intact until such time as proper scientific
investigation of the same may be had.

Very respectfully,

(Signed)   A. C. TONNER, *Acting Commissioner.*

W. M. W.—L. M.

Following is a copy of orders sent out from the Office of Indian Affairs, October 22:

Department of the Interior,
Office of Indian Affairs, Washington, D. C.

James B. Alexander, Esq.,                                      October 22, 1904.
    Superintendent Pima Indian School,
      Sacaton, Arizona.

Sir:        *       *       *       *

It has been and is the policy of this office to prevent all unauthorized persons from entering Indian reservations and despoiling historic or prehistoric ruins and taking therefrom any relics or remains of antiquity whatever. To this end your predecessors in office or perhaps you have heretofore been advised of the wishes of this office in this respect and requested to take such action as might be necessary to the end that proper protection should be afforded in the premises and all spoliation of these valuable ruins be prevented.

*       *       *       *

It is desired that you take this matter up and issue such orders or instructions and take such action as may be necessary to carry out the wishes of this office as heretofore expressed. Should you have Indian police under your charge, they should be properly cautioned and instructed. Further, reliable and trustworthy chiefs and headmen of the tribe might likewise be advised of the desire of this office to protect these remains of antiquity from being despoiled by curio hunters, etc., and directed to aid you so far as possible in the matter.

Should unauthorized persons be found on the reservation or reservations under your charge and engaged in the work of excavating or collecting relics, etc., they should be removed from the reservation and the facts in the case be reported to this office in full.

Very respectfully,
(Signed)    A. C. TONNER, *Acting Commissioner.*

W. M. W.—L. M.

Identical orders were sent at the same time to superintendents of Indian schools, agents, and additional farmers throughout New Mexico, Arizona and Colorado. These orders cover about one-fourth of all the southwestern ruins. It will be seen that these various sets of orders from the two departments embrace practically all of the ruins that are not under private ownership.

It definitely mobilizes, so to speak, a force of forest supervisors, rangers, special agents, Indian school superintendents and teachers,

Indian agents, farmers, and police, and even enlists the Indians themselves, a particularly sagacious step, in the protection of these ruins for the avowed purposes of preserving them for scientific investigation. It establishes the broad and liberal policy that any competent scientist, who desires to place the material secured in a reputable public museum, will be authorized by the Department of the Interior to examine ruins, but that no person will be permitted to enter and excavate them for the purpose of acquiring specimens for traffic or private gain, and that willful destruction of valuable historic and prehistoric landmarks must cease.

In reply to a letter addressed to Mr. W. H. Holmes, chief of the Bureau of American Ethnology, inquiring what steps were being taken by that bureau with a view to putting the Interior Department in possession of information that would be helpful in carrying out the policy of the department relative to the southwestern ruins, I received the following communication:

> Smithsonian Institution,
> Bureau of American Ethnology,
> Washington, D. C.
>
> November 19, 1904.
>
> My dear Mr. Hewett:
>
> I beg to acknowledge the receipt of your letter of the 16th instant, making inquiries regarding the steps now being taken by the Bureau of American Ethnology in furnishing information to the Interior Department relative to the location, character, and condition of the various historic and prehistoric ruins of the Southwest.
>
> In reply I have to say that much progress has been made in the preparation of maps and descriptive lists of the various archeological sites of the Pueblo region. The Bureau has been conducting explorations among these sites at frequent intervals ever since its foundation, and has published numerous reports and maps embodying the results of its researches. The preparation of a general archeological map has been in hand for several years, and the data amassed is laid down on the Geological Survey maps, upwards of fifty of the topographical sheets covering parts of Utah, Colorado, New Mexico and Arizona having been utilized in this manner.
>
> Accompanying the maps is a card catalogue of the sites, giving more or less complete data relative to the ruins and other remains. Recently a demand for this class of information has arisen in the Interior Department, and in order to properly meet this demand the work has been taken up afresh

and reliable information from all sources is being brought together. The data previously collected is now being transferred to the latest editions of the maps on which we are laying down all Indian Reserves, private land grants, and township and section lines. Distinctive symbols are used for the various classes of remains, thus aiding in identification of particular sites; and the catalogue as recently remodeled, embodies a wide range of information, especially such as is likely to be of service to the Interior Department. The work is rapidly covering all the public lands on which archeological remains of importance occur and progress maps will soon be submitted for publication. Copies of these will, if deemed advisable, be placed in the hands of land surveyors, Indian agents, custodians of reservations, teachers, and others employed in the region or having knowledge of its ancient ruins, in order that all possible additions may be made.

It is expected that in a few years the record of our more important antiquities, already completed and published for the Mississippi Valley and the Gulf states, will be extended to cover the entire country.

I am enclosing herewith samples of the catalogue cards recently introduced. They provide spaces for recording data as follows: State, county, township, range, section, drainage; map (name of sheet), number of site, class or kind of remains, common or aboriginal name, where such exist, people, if known; needs of protection, of custodianship and repair; availability for research; history and bibliography.

The information thus gathered will be available for use by the Interior Department at an early date, although the data with respect to many important sites will necessarily be imperfect.

Very truly yours,

(Signed)   W. H. HOLMES, *Chief*.

Mr. Edgar L. Hewett,
*U. S. National Museum.*

Most archeologists will agree with Governor Richards that this subject calls for some judicious legislation, but they will be especially gratified to know that, pending such enactment, an efficient and economical policy has been developed in the Department of the Interior which is being made operative as promptly as circumstances will permit. The main thing, a system of governmental protection of archeological remains, is manifestly an accomplished fact, as much so, and after the same manner, as is the protection of timber on public lands. It will be effective just so far as the commissioners of the General Land Office and of Indian Affairs are furnished with means adequate to carry the system into effect. It would now seem that all concerned can best serve the interests of science and of the public by upholding this wise policy. I would further suggest that all workers in the southwestern field should make it their duty to keep the Department of the Interior informed of violations of the above orders which come to their notice and that they should henceforth refuse to purchase for museums any specimens or collections that are not seucred by parties duly authorized to collect the same by the Secretary of the Interior. A specimen not secured by legitimate authority and not accompanied by authentic record should have no place in a reputable museum.

The bill proposed by Commissioner Richards as a substitute for all the pending bills on the subject is embodied in his annual report for 1904 to the Secretary of the Interior which can doubtless be had by addressing him. I regard it as a sound measure which provides in a simple and direct way for the end to be accomplished, and which should precede any further special enactments.

Las Vegas, New Mexico.                    EDGAR L. HEWETT.


## PRESERVATION OF ANTIQUITIES [1]

More people have visited the prehistoric ruins of the Southwest during the present season than during any five previous years. This points to a marked revival of interest in American archeology, and to the necessity for an unremitting campaign for the preservation of our antiquities. Had it not been for the activity of the General Land Office, the Office of Indian Affairs, and the Bureau of Forestry during last year, there would have been an increased amount of vandalism among the ruins. Happily the policy of the Government with reference to these matters has become fairly well known and is generally respected. Almost no collections of prehistoric material are now exposed for sale in New Mexico; but so much cannot be said for Arizona.

As the spoliation of ruins upon the public domain becomes more and more restricted by governmental authority, it becomes apparent

1. Reprinted from *American Anthropologist,* n. s., vol. 7, Oct.-Dec., 1905, pp. 569-570.

that the presence of extensive ruins on lands open to settlement adds much to their desirability as homesteads, since these antiquities may be made a source of revenue. Accordingly homesteads are sometimes located with a view solely to the acquisition of valuable ruins, with no intention of improvement and with no possibility of agriculture. Nothing but the most liberal interpretation of our homestead laws can construe such an entry as anything but fraudulent. No obstacles should be thrown in the way of bona-fide settlers who homestead the lands of the Southwest "for the purpose of actual settlement and improvement," but the gift of the lands alone is all that is contemplated and this is offered under the assumption that the settler will assist in the development of the country. It is negligence inexcusable if we continue to allow these priceless ruins to pass to individual ownership, or to give them away to be destroyed outright or excavated by unscientific methods and their contents scattered and lost. Some method should be devised whereby ruins situated on unappropriated public lands would never be alienated and at the same time no desirable agricultural land be withheld from entry. The Commissioner of the General Land Office should be empowered to withhold from any homestead entry small parcels of land on which antiquities are situated which in his judgment are of sufficient importance to warrant preservation. At present there is no law permitting him to do this. Congress must be looked to for such authority.

*Gran Quivira*—A conspicuous example of the alienation of important archeological sites through the operation of the homestead laws is that of Tabira, popularly known as "Gran Quivira," in eastern Socorro county, New Mexico. A homestead entry was filed some years ago on the quarter-section of land upon which are situated the ruins of this pueblo. This was the most extensive of the Piro settlements and is the best preserved of all the Piro ruins. Its situation on the eastern frontier of the Pueblo region renders it of unusual importance. No collections of any importance have been made from the ruins of that region. After a long contest this homestead has recently been declared valid and a patent issued to the claimant.

*Pajarito Park*—By executive order of July 29, 1905, an additional reservation of about 33,000 acres has been given to the Santa

Clara Indians. This extension embraces all of the great Puye or Santa Clara group of cliff-dwellings, the principle center of interest in the proposed Pajarito National Park. There can be no question as to the justice of this extension. It is merely giving the Indians a part of what already belonged to them by virtue of the grant of 90,000 acres by the crown of Spain to the Santa Clara pueblo in 1727, which was confirmed by Governor General Cachupin in his decree of 1763. The restitution of even a part of this land to the Indians must be commended. It is to be regretted, however, that the Indians were not offered in lieu of the few sections containing the most important ruins, other lands equally valuable for timber and grazing, and this great group of prehistoric ruins, which many travelers have asserted would be the most attractive of all our national parks, held by the Government for the benefit of the public. As it is, the national park proposition will probably be abandoned. The Indian Office will provide for the preservation of the ruins. Fortunately the other groups of ruins of the Pajarito Plateau are brought within the recently proclaimed Jemez forest reserve, so that their protection and preservation are assured.

EDGAR L. HEWETT

## PRESERVATION OF AMERICAN ANTIQUITIES [1]

### Progress During the Last Year—Needed Legislation

Prior to 1904 the only act of our Government looking toward the preservation of our antiquities was the reservation and restoration, by act of Congress of March 2, 1889, of the Casa Grande ruin in Arizona. During the last fifteen months a definite policy of preservation has rapidly developed, so that at present it may be said that approximately three-fourths of all the remains of antiquity that are situated on lands owned or controlled by the United States are under custodianship more or less efficient, and that the despoliation of ruins for commercial purposes is in a fair way to be stamped out. Following are the various steps that have been taken:

1. Reprinted from *American Anthropologist*, n. s., Vol. 8, No. 1, Jan.-March, 1906.

1. All ruins that are situated on the national forest reserves have been placed under the care of forest rangers and all unauthorized excavation or collecting prohibited. Forest rangers are clothed with power to arrest offenders, accordingly all ruins so situated are adequately policed. This is a rapidly growing class, as forest reserves are being created constantly in the Southwest, where antiquities are most numerous. Already about fifty percent of the southwestern ruins are within the limits of forest reserves and in time from two-thirds to three-fourths of them will be included. The Forest Service now protects the following reserves upon which important archeological remains are situated:

*In Colorado:* Montezuma forest reserve.

*In Utah:* Aquarius and Sevier forest reserves.

*In New Mexico:* Pecos, Gila, Lincoln, and Jemez forest reserves. The recently created Jemez forest reserve includes the vast archeological district of the Jemez plateau, embracing the Pajarito Park and the Chama, Gallinas, and Jemez valleys.

*In Arizona:* Grand Canyon, San Francisco Mountain, Black Mesa, Prescott, Pinal Mountains, Mt Graham, Santa Catalina, Santa Rita, and Chiricahua forest reserves.

Many other areas, equally important archeologically, have been withdrawn from sale or settlement pending examination of their forest condition. Noteworthy among these are the Rio Verde district in Arizona, the Taos district in New Mexico, and the Mesa Verde district in Colorado.

2. The Office of Indian Affairs prohibits all unauthorized excavations on Indian reservations and the carrying away of remains of antiquity. Special custodians have been appointed for the ruins in Canyon de Chelly and Canyon del Muerto on the Navaho reservation in Arizona, the Mesa Verde on the Southern Ute reservation in Colorado, and the Zuñi reservation in New Mexico. Indian traders on reservations are prohibited from dealing in prehistoric wares, thus removing from the Indians and other persons the temptation to despoil ruins for the sake of the small profits to be derived therefrom. This corrects one of the most prevalent and disastrous of

abuses. The most extensive archeological districts that come under the custodianship of the Indian Office are—

*In Colorado:* The Southern Ute reservation.

*In New Mexico:* The Zuñi and the Santa Clara reservations, and the various Pueblo grants.

*In Arizona:* The Navaho, Hopi, San Carlos, Walapai, Gila River, and Papago reservations.

Probably twenty-five percent of the southwestern ruins are so situated.

3.   The General Land Office holds under withdrawal, awaiting congressional action, the following important archeological districts:

*In Colorado:* The Mesa Verde district.

*In New Mexico:* The Chaco Canyon and Petrified Forest districts, and El Morro or Inscription Rock.

The ruins situated on unappropriated public lands are held to be subject to the authority of the Department of the Interior, and orders have been issued prohibiting unauthorized excavations.

In addition to these measures for the preservation of the ruins it has become necessary for the departments to formulate some mode of procedure with reference to excavation privileges. In passing on the application of the Southwest Society of the Archaeological Institute of America for such privilege, the Office of Indian Affairs held—

> . . . It is not satisfied that the Department could legally grant permission to persons or organizations to enter reservations for the purpose of excavating for and carrying away objects of archaeological value unless collecting for or under the supervision of the Government. . . .
>
> It is recommended that permission be granted the Southwest Society of the Archaeological Institute of America to conduct archaeological exploration and make excavations on Indian reservations in the Southwest upon the condition that such work is to be done under the oversight of, and in coöperation with, the Bureau of American Ethnology.

The essentials of a plan prepared in order to meet the requirements of the Office of Indian Affairs in this case and to provide for effective cooperation and avoid duplication or conflict of work are as follows:

1.   That this Society shall file with the Bureau of American Ethnology a brief but measurably definite plan of the explorations proposed on the Indian reservations, designating the person who is to have immediate charge of the field work.

2.   That it shall furnish data for use in compiling the card catalogue of antiquities now in preparation by your Bureau [the Bureau of American Ethnology] and for properly mapping the sites of the explorations and excavations.

3.   That it shall adopt a liberal policy of exchange, to the end that each participating institution may share in the benefits of the others.

4.   (a) That thorough work shall be done on each site occupied; (b) that full notes shall be taken for a catalogue of American antiquities; and (c) that the results obtained by all expeditions shall be made known within a reasonable time through published reports.

This plan was adopted by both the Office of Indian Affairs and the Forest Service and was accepted as entirely satisfactory by the Southwest Society. The departments concerned have consistently held that excavations may be conducted only for the advancement of the knowledge of archeology and not for commercial purposes. Collections may be made only for permanent preservation in public museums, and permits will be issued only to qualified archeologists who are under the direction of reputable institutions or societies. Recognizing the necessity for expert advice as to the issuance of excavation permits, the departments have adopted the plan of referring all applications for such permits to the chief of the Bureau of American Ethnology for an opinion as to the standing of the institution desiring the privilege and the competence of the archeologist who is to be in charge of the work. The spirit in which the Bureau has responded to this duty imposed on it by the departments is reflected in a letter from its chief, Mr William H. Holmes, in relation to the application of the Southwest Society of the Archaeological Institute of America, from which I quote:

> In the way of report on these inquiries I beg to state that the Archaeological Institute of America is to be classed among the most enlightened bodies of students of human history and antiquity in the country, and its component

societies, organized in various cities, include in their membership the leading archeologists of the country. It may be safely assumed that the Southwest Society, which is the largest of the allied organizations, has among its members persons fully qualified to undertake the work proposed, and that it will be wise enough to entrust the work to such, and only such, as can be implicitly relied upon to conduct the excavations in a scientific manner, to properly record observations, and to care for the collections obtained.

This Bureau appreciates fully the attitude of the Indian Office in its endeavor to preserve the national antiquities for the nation, and to prevent unauthorized and unscientific explorations; but it takes the view that whatever materials are intelligently collected and placed in reasonably protected public museums, wherever situated, that provide systematic and permanent custodianship, are preserved for all the people. The field of American archeology is a vast one, and the larger the number of properly qualified institutions that engage in the work, the better for history and science. The system of exchanges of specimens and replicas of important objects arranged between the National Museum and other museums of the country, and the well-established practice of collaboration on the part of curators and students generally, place the collections of one institution practically at the service of all.

On the whole it would appear that the system as developed secures practically what our students have been asking for; that the preservation of American antiquities is in a fair way to be accomplished, and that in the matter of excavation privileges substantial justice is being done to all. It is manifestly impossible to concentrate the entire authority in this matter in any one department. The purposes for which the lands of the United States are administered are so diverse that no department could safely undertake to grant privileges of any sort upon lands under the jurisdiction of another department. Accordingly, if archeological work is proposed on forest reserves the application for permission must be to the Secretary of Agriculture; if on a military reservation, to the Secretary of War; and if on an Indian reservation or on unappropriated public lands, to the Secretary of the Interior. Any other system would lead to great confusion and conflict of interests.

It remains to be considered what is needed in the way of national legislation on this subject. I beg leave to submit for your consideration the following memorandum of provisions which seem to be needed. They are drawn from measures previously brought forward, with such modifications as have become necessary through the rise of new conditions, and the addition of some new matter, designed to meet conditions with which we were previously unacquainted. Every effort has been made to preserve the exact spirit of the measure agreed upon last year by these two organizations (the Archaeological Institute of America and the American Anthropological Association) and at the same time meet the wishes of the various departments of the Government that will be charged with the administration of the law:

1. That any person who shall appropriate, excavate, injure, or destroy any historic or prehistoric ruin or monument, or any object of antiquity situated on lands owned or controlled by the Government of the United States, without the permission of the secretary of the department of government having jurisdiction over the lands on which said antiquities are situated should, upon conviction, be fined in a sum not more than five hundred dollars or be imprisoned for a period of not more than ninety days, or should suffer both fine and imprisonment in the discretion of the court.

2. That the President of the United States should be authorized, in his discretion, to declare by public proclamation historic landmarks, historic and prehistoric structures, and other objects of historic or scientific interest that are situated upon the lands owned or controlled by the Government of the United States to be national monuments, and to reserve as a part thereof parcels of land, the limits of which in all cases should be confined to the smallest area compatible with the proper care and management of the objects to be protected: *Provided,* That when such objects are situated upon a tract covered by a bona fide unperfected claim or held in private ownership, that tract, or so much thereof as may be necessary for the proper care and management of the object may be relinquished to the Government, and the Secretary of the Interior should be authorized to accept the relinquishment of such tracts in behalf of the Government of the United States.

3. That permits for the examination of ruins, the excavation of archeological sites, and the gathering of objects of antiquity upon the lands under their respective jurisdictions, should be granted by the Secretaries of the Interior, Agriculture, and War, to institutions which they may deem properly qualified to conduct such examination, excavation, or gathering subject to such rules and regulations as they may prescribe: *Provided,* That the examinations, excavations, and gatherings are undertaken for the benefit of reputable museums, universities, colleges, or other recognized scientific or educational institutions, with a view to increasing the knowledge of such objects, and that the gatherings shall be made for permanent preservation in public museums.

4. That the secretaries of the departments aforesaid should make and publish from time to time uniform rules and regulations for the purpose of carrying out the provisions of this law.

In a separate resolution I desire to ask these two organizations to consider the matter of the proposed Mesa Verde National Park in Colorado, provided for in a bill introduced by Representative H. M. Hogg, now pending before the national Congress. This is one of the most important pieces of legislation looking toward the preservation of American antiquities that has ever been proposed, and it seems most fitting that these organizations should give it their enthusiastic support.

[The recommendations made by Mr. Hewett in the above paper were subsequently considered at the joint business meeting of the Archaeological Institute of America and the American Anthropological Association, were unanimously accepted, and subsequently embodied in a bill which has been introduced by the Honorable John F. Lacey of Iowa as H. R. 11016. A resolution was also passed urging the creation of the Mesa Verde National Park in Colorado.— *Editor.*]

Washington, D. C., *December,* 1905.

## [PUBLIC—No. 209.]

An Act For the preservation of American antiquities.

*Be it enacted by the Senate and House of Representatives of the United States of America in Congress assembled,* That any person who shall appropriate, excavate, injure, or destroy any historic or prehistoric ruin or monument, or any object of antiquity, situated on lands owned or controlled by the Government of the United States, without the permission of the Secretary of the Department of the Government having jurisdiction over the lands on which said antiquities are situated, shall, upon conviction, be fined in a sum of not more than five hundred dollars or be imprisoned for a period of not more than ninety days, or shall suffer both fine and imprisonment, in the discretion of the court.

Sec. 2. That the President of the United States is hereby authorized, in his discretion, to declare by public proclamation historic landmarks, historic and prehistoric structures, and other objects of historic or scientific interest that are situated upon the lands owned or controlled by the Government of the United States to be national monuments, and may reserve as a part thereof parcels of land, the limits of which in all cases shall be confined to the smallest area compatible with the proper care and management of the objects to be protected: *Provided,* That when such objects are situated upon a tract covered by a bona fide unperfected claim or held in private ownership, the tract, or so much thereof as may be necessary for the proper care and management of the object, may be relinquished to the Government, and the Secretary of the Interior is hereby authorized to accept the relinquishment of such tracts in behalf of the Government of the United States.

Sec. 3. That permits for the examination of ruins, the excavation of archaeological sites, and the gathering of objects of antiquity upon the lands under their respective jurisdictions may be granted by the Secretaries of the Interior, Agriculture, and War to institutions which they may deem properly qualified to conduct such examination, excavation, or gathering, subject to such rules and regulations as they may prescribe: *Provided,* That the examinations, excavations, and gatherings are undertaken for the benefit of reputable museums, universities, colleges, or other recognized scientific or educational institutions, with a view to increasing the knowledge of such objects, and that the gatherings shall be made for permanent preservation in public museums.

Sec. 4. That the Secretaries of the Departments aforesaid shall make and publish from time to time uniform rules and regulations for the purpose of carrying out the provisions of this Act.

Approved, June 8, 1906.

NOTE: A letter from the Department of the Interior, National Park Service, under date of December 27, 1937, states that the law of 1906 and the rules and regulations prescribed for its operation remain in effect as originally adopted.—E. L. H.

## UNIFORM RULES AND REGULATIONS

Prescribed by the Secretaries of the Interior, Agriculture, and War
to Carry Out the Provisions of the "Act for the Preservation of American Antiquities," Approved June
8, 1906 (34 Stat. L., 225).

1. Jurisdiction over ruins, archeological sites, historic and prehistoric monuments and structures, objects of antiquity, historic landmarks, and other objects of historic or scientific interest, shall be
exercised under the act by the respective Departments as follows:

By the Secretary of Agriculture over lands within the exterior
limits of forest reserves, by the Secretary of War over lands within
the exterior limits of military reservations, by the Secretary of the
Interior over all other lands owned or controlled by the Government
of the United States, provided the Secretaries of War and Agriculture
may by agreement cooperate with the Secretary of the Interior in the
supervision of such monuments and objects covered by the act of
June 8, 1906, as may be located on lands near or adjacent to forest
reserves and military reservations, respectively.

2. No permit for the removal of any ancient monument or
structure which can be permanently preserved under the control of the
United States *in situ,* and remain an object of interest, shall be granted.

3. Permits for the examination of ruins, the excavation of
archeological sites, and the gathering of objects of antiquity will be
granted, by the respective Secretaries having jurisdiction, to reputable
museums, universities, colleges, or other recognized scientific or educational institutions, or to their duly authorized agents.

4. No exclusive permits shall be granted for a larger area than
the applicant can reasonably be expected to explore fully and systematically within the time limit named in the permit.

5. Each application for a permit should be filed with the Secretary having jurisdiction, and must be accompanied by a definite outline
of the proposed work, indicating the name of the institution making

the request, the date proposed for beginning the field work, the length of time proposed to be devoted to it, and the person who will have immediate charge of the work. The application must also contain an exact statement of the character of the work, whether examination, excavation, or gathering, and the public museum in which the collections made under the permit are to be permanently preserved. The application must be accompanied by a sketch plan or description of the particular site or area to be examined, excavated, or searched, so definite that it can be located on the map with reasonable accuracy.

6. No permit will be granted for a period of more than three years, but if the work has been diligently prosecuted under the permit, the time may be extended for proper cause upon application.

7. Failure to begin work under a permit within six months after it is granted, or failure to diligently prosecute such work after it has been begun, shall make the permit void without any order or proceeding by the Secretary having jurisdiction.

8. Applications for permits shall be referred to the Smithsonian Institution for recommendation.

9. Every permit shall be in writing and copies shall be transmitted to the Smithsonian Institution and the field officer in charge of the land involved. The permittee will be furnished with a copy of these rules and regulations.

10. At the close of each season's field work the permittee shall report in duplicate to the Smithsonian Institution, in such form as its secretary may prescribe, and shall prepare in duplicate a catalogue of the collections and of the photographs made during the season, indicating therein such material, if any, as may be available for exchange.

11. Institutions and persons receiving permits for excavation shall, after the completion of the work, restore the lands upon which they have worked to their customary condition, to the satisfaction of the field officer in charge.

12. All permits shall be terminable at the discretion of the Secretary having jurisdiction.

13. The field officer in charge of land owned or controlled by the Government of the United States shall, from time to time, inquire and report as to the existence, on or near such lands, of ruins and archeological sites, historic or prehistoric ruins or monuments, objects of antiquity, historic landmarks, historic and prehistoric structures, and other objects of historic or scientific interest.

14. The field officer in charge may at all times examine the permit of any person or institution claiming privileges granted in accordance with the act and these rules and regulations, and may fully examine all work done under such permit.

15. All persons duly authorized by the Secretaries of Agriculture, War, and Interior may apprehend or cause to be arrested, as provided in the act of February 6, 1905 (33 Stat. L., 700), any person or persons who appropriate, excavate, injure, or destroy any historic or prehistoric ruin or monument, or any object of antiquity on lands under the supervision of the Secretaries of Agriculture, War, and Interior, respectively.

16. Any object of antiquity taken, or collection made, on lands owned or controlled by the United States, without a permit, as prescribed by the act and these rules and regulations, or there taken or made, contrary to the terms of the permit, or contrary to the act and these rules and regulations, may be seized wherever found and at any time, by the proper field officer or by any person duly authorized by the Secretary having jurisdiction, and disposed of as the Secretary shall determine, by deposit in the proper national depository or otherwise.

17. Every collection made under the authority of the act and of these rules and regulations shall be preserved in the public museum designated in the permit and shall be accessible to the public. No such collection shall be removed from such public museum without the written authority of the Secretary of the Smithsonian Institution, and then only to another public museum, where it shall be accessible to the public; and when any public museum, which is a depository of any collection made under the provisions of the act and these rules and regulations, shall cease to exist, every such collection in such public

museum shall thereupon revert to the national collections and be placed in the proper national depository.

---

WASHINGTON, D. C., *December 28, 1906.*

The foregoing rules and regulations are hereby approved in triplicate and, under authority conferred by law on the Secretaries of the Interior, Agriculture, and War, are hereby made and established, to take effect immediately.

E. A. HITCHCOCK,
*Secretary of the Interior.*
JAMES WILSON,
*Secretary of Agriculture.*
WM. H. TAFT,
*Secretary of War.*

The part that the State of New Mexico has taken officially in the movement for the preservation of Southwestern antiquities is set forth in the following report entitled, "Conservation of Scientific Resources of New Mexico." The long effort to secure legislation for the conservation of the scientific resources of New Mexico, especially its antiquities, was consummated in 1931 by the passage of the act which is herewith published, together with the rules and regulations under which the law will be administered:

## PREFATORY NOTE

The purpose of the laws and regulations for the conservation of the scientific resources of New Mexico is to save these assets of the state for the use and benefit of the people, and to lend all possible encouragement to scientific work. To this end the Science Commission desires to enlist all the law-enforcing machinery of the state, the aid of every citizen, and the co-operation of the Federal Government and neighboring states. It has been demonstrated that without such co-operation laws and regulations are ineffective.

The Commission will issue permits to thoroughly reputable institutions only. Such institutions will be expected to show that the employees to whom field work is to be entrusted are especially trained for the work proposed. When their enterprises are approved and inaugurated, the Commission will do everything in its power to assist, and will see that scientific work is unhampered by unnecessary restrictions. It believes that institutions seeking to operate in New Mexico will appreciate the above purposes and will cordially co-operate in carrying them out.

•

## AN ACT
## FOR THE PRESERVATION OF THE SCIENTIFIC RESOURCES OF NEW MEXICO

*Senate Steering Committee Substitute for House Bill No. 124*

Tenth Legislature of New Mexico, Laws of New Mexico, 1931
Chapter 42, Page 81

*Be It Enacted by the Legislature of the State of New Mexico:*

SECTION 1.   That any person who shall appropriate, excavate, injure, or destroy any historic or prehistoric ruin or monument, or any object of historical, archaeological or scientific value, situated on lands owned or controlled by the State of New Mexico, or its institutions, without the recommendation of the Science Commission hereinafter created, and the consent of the Commissioner of the State Land Office, shall be fined in a sum of not more than $500.00 or be imprisoned for a period of not more than ninety days, or shall suffer both fine and imprisonment in the discretion of the court; and it shall be the duty of any employee of the State Land Office, or any peace officer, including constables and sheriffs, to proceed against any violation of this law, and the duty of district attorneys of this state to prosecute any one violating the provisions of this Act.

SEC. 2.   That the Commissioner of the State Land Office is hereby authorized on recommendation of the above named Science Commission with the approval of the Commissioner of Public Lands to declare by public proclamation that historic and prehistoric structures and other objects of scientific interest that are situated upon the lands owned or controlled by the State of New Mexico, shall be state monuments, and may reserve as a part thereof such parcels of land as may be necessary to the proper care and management of the objects to be protected.

SEC. 3. That permits for the examination of ruins, the excavation of archaeological sites, and the gathering of objects of antiquity, or general scientific interest, may be granted by the Commissioner of Public Lands on recommendation of the Science Commission to institutions which they may deem properly qualified to conduct such examination, excavation, or gathering, subject to such rules and regulations as the aforesaid Commission with the approval of the Commissioner of Public Lands may proscribe; *Provided,* that the examinations and gatherings are undertaken for the benefit of reputable museums, universities, colleges, or other recognized scientific or educational institutions, with a view of increasing the knowledge of such objects, and; *Provided,* that not less than fifty per cent of all specimens so collected by non-resident institutions shall be retained as the property of the State of New Mexico, unless the Commissioner of Public Lands shall expressly accept a smaller proportion, as meeting the requirements of this Act, and; *Provided,* that this Act shall not interfere with the making of natural history collections by individuals for scientific purposes only, provided that such individuals secure permits as prescribed in this section.

SEC. 4. Unless other locations be designated by the Commission, the Museum of New Mexico shall be the depository for all collections made under the provisions of this Act and shall distribute material from such collections to local museums throughout the State of New Mexico on request of the governing bodies of the said local museums, when in the opinion of the Science Commission, proper arrangements are made for the safe custodianship and public exhibition of such material.

SEC. 5. The disposition of historic and scientific material referred to in this Act, to individuals or institutions outside the State of New Mexico, is expressly forbidden, except by permission of the Science Commission, approved by the Commissioner of Public Lands, and the transportation by public or private carriers of such material to points outside the State of New Mexico is expressly prohibited, except as may be necessary in carrying out the provisions of the permits issued by the Government of the United States under the Federal Statute for the Preservation of American Antiquities, and under the permits granted by the Science Commission of the State of New Mexico.

SEC. 6.   That for the purpose of carrying out the provisions of the Act, there is hereby created a body to be known as the Science Commission of New Mexico, which shall be composed of the following heads of the State Educational and Scientific Institutions, viz.: the Presidents of the University of New Mexico, the New Mexico College of Agriculture and Mechanic Arts, the New Mexico School of Mines, the Normal Schools of New Mexico, the Director of the Museum of New Mexico, the Superintendent of the New Mexico Military Institute and the State Superintendent of Public Instruction.  Said Commission by and with the advice and consent of the Commissioner of Public Lands shall make and publish from time to time uniform rules and regulations for the purpose of carrying out the provisions of this Act and shall perform all the duties prescribed herein without pay.

SEC. 7.   That all Acts or parts of Acts in conflict with or within the purview of this Act, are hereby repealed.

Attest:

R. H. POOLER,
    Chief Clerk of the Senate.

Signed: A. W. HOCKENHULL,
    Pres. of Senate.

Attest:

GEO. W. ARMIJO,
    Chief Clerk of House of Rep.

ALVAN N. WHITE,
    Speaker of the House
    of Representatives.

Approved by me this 14th day of March, 1931.

ARTHUR SELIGMAN,
    Governor of New Mexico.

Filed in the Office of Secretary of State of New Mexico,
    at 11:00 A. M., March 16, 1931.
Signed: MRS. M. P. BACA, Secretary.

## RULES AND REGULATIONS

*Prescribed by the Science Commission of New Mexico With the Approval of the Commissioner of the State Land Office, to Carry Out the Provisions of the "Act for the Preservation of the Scientific Resources of New Mexico," Passed by the Tenth Legislature of New Mexico, Chapter 42, Page 81, Laws of New Mexico, 1931*

1. Permits for the examination of ruins, the excavation of archaeological sites, and the gathering of objects of antiquity or of historic or scientific value will be granted by the Commissioner of Public Lands on recommendation of the State Science Commission to reputable museums, universities, colleges, or other recognized scientific or educational institutions.

2. Each application for a permit should be filed with the Secretary of the Science Commission and must be accompanied by an outline of the proposed work, indicating the name of the institution making the request, the date proposed for beginning the field work, the length of time proposed to be devoted to it, the person who will have immediate charge of the work, and his professional qualifications. The application must also contain a statement of the character of the work, and the institution in which the collections made under the permit are to be permanently preserved.

3. No permit shall be granted for the removal of any ancient monument or object of scientific interest which can be permanently preserved *in situ,* and remain an object of interest.

4. Permits will normally be granted for periods up to three years, and for projects of exceptional importance this limit may be modified by the Science Commission.

5. No exclusive permit shall be granted for a larger area than the applicant can reasonably be expected to explore fully and systematically within the time limit named in the permit.

6. Failure to begin work under a permit within six months after it is granted, or failure to prosecute diligently such work after it has been begun, shall make the permit void, upon recommendation of the Science Commission.

7. At the close of each season's field work the permittee shall report in duplicate to the Science Commission in such form as its secretary may prescribe, accompanied by a catalogue of the collections made and examples of photographs made during the season.

8. All permits shall be terminable by the Commissioner of Public Lands on recommendation of the Science Commission.

9. The Science Commission or its agent may at all times examine the permit of any person or institution operating under this Act and these rules and regulations, and may fully examine all work done and all collections made under such permit. The secretary of the Science Commission may at all times be called upon by permittees or their agents for advice or co-operation in connection with the work.

10. Any object of scientific interest taken or collections made, on lands owned or controlled by the State of New Mexico without a permit as prescribed by the act and these rules and regulations, or contrary to the terms of the permit, or contrary to the act and these rules and regulations, may be seized, wherever found and at any time, by the proper authorities of the State of New Mexico on request of the Science Commission.

11. Every collection made under the authority of the act and of these rules and regulations shall be preserved in the institution designated in the permit, and shall be accessible to the public. No such collection shall be removed from such institution without the written authority of the Secretary of the Science Commission and then only to another institution where it shall be accessible to the public; and when any public museum which is the depository of any collection made under the provisions of the act and these rules and regulations shall cease to exist, every such collection in such institution shall thereupon revert to the Museum of New Mexico for such disposition as may be ordered by the Science Commission.

*Signed:* Executive Committee of the New Mexico Science Commission

A. O. BOWDEN, *President*

REGINALD G. FISHER, *Executive Secretary.*

E. H. WELLS, *Third Committee Member.*

Approved: Date March 3, 1932.

J. F. HINKLE, *Commissioner of Public Lands of New Mexico.*

(Seal)

*Index*

# INDEX